NATIONS *IN TRANSITION*

TAIWAN

NATIONS *IN TRANSITION*

TAIWAN

by Robert Green

GREENHAVEN PRESS®

THOMSON

™

GALE

San Diego • Detroit • New York • San Francisco • Cleveland
New Haven, Conn. • Waterville, Maine • London • Munich

LIBRARY OF CONGRESS CATALOGING-IN-PUBLICATION DATA

Green, Robert.
  Taiwan / by Robert Green.
    v. cm. — (Nations in transition)
  Contents: On the edge of the Middle Kingdom—A republic in exile—The other China—
Economic and social transformation—In search of normalcy
  Includes bibliographical references and index.
    ISBN 0-7377-1281-3 (alk. paper)
    1. Taiwan—Politics and government—1988—-Juvenile literature. 2. Taiwan—
Economic policy—1975—-Juvenile literature. [1. Taiwan.] I. Title. II. Nations in
transition (Greenhaven Press)
    DS799.847.G74 2004
    951.24'905—dc22

                                                          2003013731

Contents

Foreword

In 1986 Soviet general secretary Mikhail Gorbachev initiated his plan to reform the economic, political, and social structure of the Soviet Union. Nearly three-quarters of a century of Communist ideology was dismantled in the next five years. As the totalitarian regime relaxed its rule and opened itself up to the West, the Soviet peoples clamored for more freedoms. Hard-line Communists resisted Gorbachev's lead, but glasnost, or "openness," could not be stopped with the will of the common people behind it.

In 1991 the changing USSR held its first multicandidate elections. The reform-minded Boris Yeltsin, a supporter of Gorbachev, became the first popularly elected president of the Russian Republic in Soviet history. Under Yeltsin's leadership, the old Communist policies soon all but disintegrated, as did the Soviet Union itself. The Union of Soviet Socialist Republics broke apart into fifteen independent entities. The former republics reformed into a more democratic union now referred to as the Commonwealth of Independent States. Russia remained the nominal figurehead of the commonwealth, but it no longer dictated the future of the other independent states.

By the new millennium, Russia and the other commonwealth states still faced crises. The new states were all in transition from decades of totalitarian rule to the postglasnost era of unprecedented and untested democratic reforms. Revamping the Soviet economy may have opened up new opportunities in private ownership of property and business, but it did not bring overnight prosperity to the former republics. Common necessities such as food still remain in short supply in many regions. And while new governments seek to stabilize their authority, crime rates have escalated throughout the former Soviet Union. Still, the people are confident that their newfound freedoms—freedom of speech and assembly, freedom of religion, and even the right of workers to strike—will ultimately better their lives. The process of change will take time and the people are willing to see their respective states through the challenges of this transitional period in Soviet history.

The collapse and rebuilding of the former Soviet Union provides perhaps the best example of a contemporary "nation in transition," the focus of this Greenhaven Press series. However, other nations that fall under the series rubric have faced a host of unique and varied cultural shifts. India, for instance, is a stable, guiding force in Asia, yet it remains a nation in transition more than fifty years after winning independence from Great Britain. The entire infrastructure of the Indian subcontinent still bears the marking of its colonial past: In a land of eighteen official spoken languages, for example, English remains the voice of politics and education. India is still coming to grips with its colonial legacy while forging its place as a strong player in Asian and world affairs.

North Korea's place in Greenhaven's Nations in Transition series is based on major recent political developments. After decades of antagonism between its Communist government and the democratic leadership of South Korea, tensions seemed to ease in the late 1990s. Even under the shadow of the North's developing nuclear capabilities, the presidents of both North and South Korea met in 2000 to propose plans for possible reunification of the two estranged nations. And though it is one of the three remaining bastions of communism in the world, North Korea is choosing not to remain an isolated relic of the Cold War. While it has not earned the trust of the United States and many of its Western allies, North Korea has begun to reach out to its Asian neighbors to encourage trade and cultural exchanges.

These three countries exemplify the types of changes and challenges that qualify them as subjects of study in the Greenhaven Nations in Transition series. The series examines specific nations to disclose the major social, political, economic, and cultural shifts that have caused massive change and in many cases, brought about regional and/or worldwide shifts in power. Detailed maps, inserts, and pictures help flesh out the people, places, and events that define the country's transitional period. Furthermore, a comprehensive bibliography points readers to other sources that will deepen their understanding of the nation's complex past and contemporary struggles. With these tools, students and casual readers trace both past history and future challenges of these important nations.

Introduction
A New Democracy

In May 2000, voters in the Republic of China, known more commonly around the globe as Taiwan, went to the polls. A great deal was at stake. The shackles of martial law had been loosened only just over a decade earlier. Voters were free to choose between two political parties representing distinct visions for the country. The election received unprecedented international media coverage. Could a nation that had never experienced a change in political

Chen Shui-bian, leader of Taiwan's Democratic Progressive Party, was elected president of the island nation in 2000.

power conduct a fair election and honor the results if the opposition party won? The world's cameras shone on the budding democracy, and ink poured forth from the pens of print journalists.

The ruling Nationalist Party, or Kuomintang (KMT), which had ruled the island for a half-century, first through martial law and more recently through elections, faced the possibility of defeat for the first time in its history. The main opposition party, the Democratic Progressive Party (DPP), whose members had suffered harassment, imprisonment, and exile when they tried to make their voices heard during the martial law period, hoped to topple their political foe through peaceful elections. When the final votes were counted, the opposition party, to the surprise of everyone and perhaps itself most of all, had won the presidency of the fledgling democracy. "Taiwan stands up, demonstrating a firmness of purpose and faith in democracy,"[1] said Chen Shui-bian, the newly elected president.

The election of the opposition leader to the presidency was hailed as a great advance for democracy in Taiwan. The once dictatorial Nationalists accepted defeat and stated that they would win back the presidency in later elections. The elections went down as one of history's rare examples of a peaceful political transition from dictatorship to democracy.

The Flash Point for War?

Amid the general interest generated by the election, two of the world's great powers riveted their attention on Taiwan: the United States, the world's sole superpower since the collapse of the Soviet Union, and China, a growing power in its own right. Both watched the election with a great deal of anxiety because they had long struggled to determine the future of the island. The mainland Chinese still claim Taiwan as a renegade province of China, and the United States arms the island to defend it from Chinese attacks in accordance with a law passed by the U.S. Congress.

Heightening the tension in the Taiwan Strait was the fact that the main opposition party, the DPP, supported an outright declaration of independence for the island nation. The mainland Chinese had repeatedly threatened to retake the island by force should it proclaim independence. The United States, in return, indicated that it would defend the island, which it considers an outpost for democracy in the Far East.

The election of a pro-independence leader, therefore, raised the specter of war in the Taiwan Strait, one of the most likely flash points for a world war. The threat of a Chinese military response to the election of Chen Shui-bian hung over the celebrations during the transfer of political power. Before the election, in fact, Chinese troops had staged military maneuvers in the Taiwan Strait that included a mock amphibious landing that could be used to retake Taiwan. The saber rattling was a heavy-handed reminder to the people of Taiwan that China would oppose any moves toward independence with force. To counter the Chinese, the United States announced that it was equally determined to assure Taiwan's sovereignty, a veiled threat to defend the island in case of a Chinese invasion. The reassurances the United States gave Taiwan somewhat blunted the effects of intimidation by the Chinese. The United States, however, also discouraged the new president of Taiwan from declaring the island's independence in order to avoid a possible war.

The election episode reflected the dangerous position of the island and its importance on the world stage. Taiwan certainly occupies one of the strangest positions in global politics. It is, in fact, not recognized as a country by most of the world, even though its citizens elect their own leaders and protect themselves with their own military. Taiwan is a nation in every respect except in the realm of international diplomacy, where it is often treated as a nominal part of China, though the two have been separated for more than fifty years. Even the United States, which risks the safety of its own sailors to ward off Chinese aggression in the Taiwan Strait, does not officially recognize Taiwan as a country.

The curious status of Taiwan is the result of the Chinese Civil War (1927–1949), during which the Nationalists and Chinese Communists battled on and off for control of mainland China. In 1949 the Nationalist armies found themselves in an untenable position and withdrew to the island of Taiwan to regroup and plan for a counterattack on the mainland.

To ensure civil obedience during this dangerous time, the Nationalist government on Taiwan ruled through martial law. The United States, a key supporter of the Nationalist government, tolerated this smothering of political freedom because Taiwan offered an alternative to Communist China. Western democracies, which had dubbed the Communist victory on the mainland the "fall" of China, relied on the Taiwanese in their island fortress to provide an advanced staging ground in the Far East for the forces of democracy. U.S. general Douglas MacArthur referred to the fortified island as an unsinkable aircraft carrier.

Because of world events, Taiwan found itself playing a role out of all proportion to the size of the country. It had become, in short, an essential ally to the Western democracies in the Cold War with Communist states and an important factor in the strategic planning of nations fighting a worldwide war of ideology.

Years of Change

Taiwan has been trapped in this diplomatic no man's land ever since. It is officially unrecognized as a nation by friend and foe. And yet progress in the country has been astonishingly rapid. The engine of the island's rapid transformation since the 1950s has been the economy.

In a short span of a few decades, the Taiwanese economy has undergone revolutionary developments. Where once the country relied predominantly on farming and fishing for its livelihood, it is today one of the world's leading exporters of high-tech goods. So rapidly did the economy modernize that Taiwan was nicknamed a "tiger economy," a term used to describe Asian economies undergoing a boom from the 1970s to the 1990s.

The rapid industrialization of Taiwan's economy led to higher standards of living, including better housing, better education, and better transportation. This in turn led to a flush of pride in being Taiwanese, and the island people began clamoring for more participation in their own political process. Martial law crumbled, and by the 1990s the people of Taiwan had acquired the right to elect their own leaders and determine their own future through democratic elections. Elections today are lively demonstrations of the people's desire to make their voices heard, and they involve some of the most fundamental questions a nation can face: Will the country proclaim independence or reunite with China? Can war with China be averted if the island chooses independence? Will the predominantly ethnic Chinese people of Taiwan forge closer economic and political links with other Chinese communities in Asia as part of greater China? Or, will the Taiwanese choose to emphasize their differences with China and continue their close relations with the United States and other nations to counterbalance Chinese pressure?

Whatever the Taiwanese decide, they are free to make their own choice through democratic elections, unhampered by the stifling restrictions of occupation and martial law that kept the majority of the population silent for most of the twentieth century.

On the Edge of the Middle Kingdom

1

Political freedom and self-determination are recent developments in Taiwan, one of the world's newest democracies. During the greater part of its history, the people of Taiwan have been unable to elect their own leaders or to establish their own governments. Although various foreign powers have governed the island, no country has determined the character of Taiwanese society as much as China, Taiwan's nearest neighbor. Ninety-eight percent of Taiwan's population is Han Chinese, the principal ethnic group of mainland China, and even today China claims Taiwan as its own.

Taiwan, even when it was not ruled directly by China, was largely developed by the Chinese. And Taiwan's geographic position on the edge of the Middle Kingdom, the Chinese name for China, resulted in a connection with the Chinese mainland that still influences Taiwan today.

Taiwan Before the Chinese

The Taiwanese have a term for the earliest Chinese inhabitants of Taiwan: the *benshengren,* or "people of this province." Yet when the Chinese began to settle the island in the fifteenth century, the island was already inhabited. The original inhabitants of Taiwan were therefore not the *benshengren* but the people known today as the aborigines, who, before the arrival of the Chinese, held sway over the entire island. Taiwan's aborigines most likely originated in Southeast Asia or the islands of the Pacific and are generally thought to be Austronesian peoples, seafaring tribes that settled in such places as Indonesia and Malaysia.

In Taiwan, the aborigines formed distinct tribes in different parts of the island. Some made a living by fishing in the waters

Taiwan's Aborigines

Long before the Chinese arrived in Taiwan, aboriginal peoples populated the island. Until recently, Taiwan's aborigines were often referred to as "Mountain People," but this misnomer only reflected the fact that the Chinese had driven them from Taiwan's fertile low-lying areas. The aborigines, in fact, once hunted and fished in the valleys of Taiwan's mountain ranges and the coastal plains as well as the inaccessible inland mountains.

Archaeological sites on Taiwan reveal settlements dating back twelve thousand to fifteen thousand years. Most scholars believe that the earliest of the aborigines to arrive on the island hailed from the Austronesian peoples who inhabited Southeast Asia and the Pacific Islands. Some scholars, however, point to later prehistoric civilizations in northern Taiwan that could possibly have originated in China.

Wherever they came from, the aborigines gained a reputation for ferocity among visitors to the island. Shipwrecked sailors and parties of explorers often first met the aborigines in the confusion of combat. Tales of hair-raising encounters with the tattooed natives of Taiwan spread among seamen of the Pacific, and the aboriginal practice of taking heads for souvenirs only bolstered the grim reputation of the island.

In later years, fear of the aborigines waned, and missionaries and scholars recorded their languages and customs. During the Japanese occupation of Taiwan (1895–1945), Japanese anthropologists became greatly interested in aboriginal culture, and traditional aboriginal artifacts such as clothing, jewelry, and weapons were much prized in Japan.

Today the descendants of Taiwan's earliest inhabitants make up less than 2 percent of the population, comprising ten tribes, each with its own distinct language and heritage. Public schools now teach classes about aboriginal culture and sometimes offer lessons in aboriginal languages. The aborigines, however, are still sometimes mistaken for foreigners by the dominant ethnically Chinese population, which makes up 98 percent of the population.

around the island, and others established villages in the mountains. The Chinese later described Taiwan's earliest inhabitants as "Mountain People," but only because they were driven from most of the low-lying regions by the Chinese immigrants. The name of one extinct tribe, the Pingpu, or "Plains Dwellers," for example, indicates that their civilization flourished on the fertile coastal plains of Taiwan.

The coastal tribes frequently resisted the intrusion of newcomers. For a time, the island was feared because seafarers whose ships foundered on Taiwan's shores were often killed by the aborigines, who sometimes took their heads for trophies. In a letter dated 1583, a Spanish missionary sailing from the city of Macao in southern China to Japan recorded his narrow escape after his ship was wrecked on the coast of Taiwan, which the Spanish called Hermosa ("Beautiful"):

> Along the way . . . is an island called Hermosa, for its tall and green mountains seen from this side are a sight lovely to behold. The Portuguese have traveled to Japan between this island and the Chinese coast for about 40 years without ever exploring or landing on it. This [the accident] we owe to the pilot's negligence. It was a Sunday at midnight. [There was a] great wind. The junk or ship which I boarded was very big and carried all of Macao's wealth because the other [boat] ahead was small and carried little cargo.
>
> We managed to get off with some planks, while others swam until they got exhausted. In short, the great junk fell into pieces and all the goods were scattered on the shore and rotted there. Later, some natives, naked and [armed] with bows and quivers, fell on us and with great spirit and determination, without hesitating and without hurting anyone, divested us of everything that we had. They came everyday, and more often at night, killing some and wounding many others with their arrows, to the point that we had to defend ourselves the best we could. We remained in this condition more than three months [feeding on] available rice until we finally finished building a small boat out of the pieces we retrieved from the large one. [2]

Despite the fierceness of the aborigines, European interest in the island that lay in the middle of vital shipping lines between Southeast Asia and Japan only increased. Starting in the fifteenth century, European ships raised their canvases and sailed to distant parts of the world. Sea captains sought new items to trade and new lands to conquer, and missionaries sought new populations among whom they could spread the Christian faith. The first European record of Taiwan comes from the log of a Portuguese ship sailing to Japan in 1517. Catching sight of the majesty of the mist-enshrouded peaks of the island, the captain named the island Ilha Formosa, the "Beautiful Island."

As competition increased in the region for control of the sea lanes, the Dutch established a base on the Pescadores, an island group known in Chinese as P'eng-hu, in the Taiwan Strait. From there they expanded to Taiwan, where they defeated Spanish settlers on the northern coast and claimed Taiwan as a colony, administered by the Dutch East India Company. Their colonial capital was established at the southern port of Tainan, where they built a fort and warehouses for their trade goods. They built another trading center with a fort to protect it in the north at Tamsui. Although the Dutch were most concerned with establishing a weigh station for the shipping in the region, they also built settlements and rented land to the increasing number of Chinese settlers sailing across the strait from China.

Taiwan Struggles for Autonomy

No culture shaped society on the island as much as that of the Chinese. Immigrants from China would eventually account for 98 percent of the population. Taiwan would be forever changed by the growing connection with the Chinese mainland, which provided the island with not only a cultural wellspring but also a lasting source of political tension.

China has suffered from overpopulation since ancient times. Although the country is vast, arable land is comparatively scarce. Moreover, droughts and floods from rivers overflowing their banks have led to frequent occurrences of famine. As a result, the Chinese, generation after generation, have struck out into the wider world in search of more room and better opportunities. Emigrants most frequently sailed from the coastal provinces of southern China, including the province of Fujian, separated from Taiwan

Cheng Ho's Voyages into the Unknown

Perhaps the most famous Chinese traveler to ever visit Taiwan was the intrepid sea captain Cheng Ho, China's most storied explorer. His life is as remarkable as his voyages, which marked the high point of Chinese navigation and exploration.

Cheng Ho, born into a family of Muslim rebels in the late fourteenth century, was captured by Chinese troops and enslaved. As a slave, he was castrated and condemned to live out his days as a eunuch. Despite his early hardships, Cheng Ho's remarkable talents caught the attention of his master, a prince of the royal family. He entrusted his servant with a military command and, with Cheng Ho's help, he seized the throne and became the Emperor Yung-lo.

To display the greatness of China, the new emperor dispatched the imperial fleet on voyages throughout Asia. Cheng Ho took command of the expeditions, and between 1405 and 1433 he led seven voyages as commander of an armada of three hundred ships. His flagship measured four hundred feet and had seven masts with billowing red silk sails that carried his twenty-eight thousand sailors into the unknown. (By comparison, the largest of Christopher Columbus's three ships measured only eighty-five feet long.)

Cheng Ho's voyages took him throughout the archipelagos of Southeast Asia, along the coast of India, to the Arabian Peninsula, and to the Horn of Africa. He brought great riches back with him and opened trade routes to many parts of Asia and beyond. In 1430 Cheng Ho was shipwrecked on Taiwan, where he received assistance from the aborigines and later presented a written account of the island to the emperor. Three years later, China's most famous sea captain died in the Indian port city of Calicut. After his death, China entered a period of isolation. Yung-lo's successor dismantled the Chinese navy and attempted to destroy all traces of Cheng Ho's voyages, believing that China had no future as a sea power.

only one hundred miles away by the waters of the Taiwan Strait. Slowly, Chinese fishermen plying the waters of the Taiwan Strait began to settle on its low-lying plains abutting Taiwan's western shores. By the time of the arrival of the Europeans during the sixteenth century, there were already significant numbers of Chinese on the island.

In Chinese records of the time, the name Taiwan occurs infrequently and the island was not considered part of the Middle Kingdom. The Chinese on Taiwan therefore lived in a hurly-burly society in which government and law were largely nonexistent. For the most part, this suited the Chinese settlers, who survived by fishing, trade, and, sometimes, piracy, escaping the notice of the imperial officials on the mainland. They also escaped the heavy burden of taxation and gained some breathing room from the crowded coastal provinces of the mainland, from which most Chinese immigrants to Taiwan came.

Events on the Chinese mainland, however, began to influence the situation in Taiwan in the mid–seventeenth century, when marauding nomadic horsemen from the steppes to the north of China threatened the rule of the Ming emperors. The Manchus, as the nomads were known, attacked an imperial administration already weakened from within. Their highly disciplined warriors, serried in ranks riding under flags of varied color, were expert with the bow and sword. These bannermen pierced the gates of the Great Wall, which was designed to protect the Chinese Empire from the northern tribes, and put down all resistance with violence. As the Ming dynasty collapsed, loyal forces moved southward to regroup and carry on the fight.

As a result, Taiwan was drawn directly into Chinese affairs for the first time in its history. To command the Ming naval forces against the northern invaders, the last Ming emperor commissioned Cheng Chih-lung, a pirate captain who raided the shipping lanes in the East and South China Seas from his base in Taiwan. Cheng proved an able imperial commander, but the navy had limited powers to stop a nomadic force galloping through the interior. The Manchus toppled the Ming and established their own dynasty, the Ch'ing, in 1644.

For some time after, the Manchus were busy subduing resistance on the mainland and adopting Chinese administrative methods to rule their new conquest. In the meantime, partisans loyal to the Ming dynasty retreated to Taiwan, where they made plans to attack the mainland. These forces were led by Cheng Ch'eng-kung, who had inherited his father's pirate fleet. The younger Cheng proved to be a fierce commander in his own right. He established a government in Taiwan modeled on the Chinese imperial bureaucracy. And he ruled over the island while his fleet frequently raided the Chinese mainland and defeated Ch'ing naval expeditions sent to destroy him. Although Cheng never succeeded in reestablishing the Ming dynasty on the mainland, he became a hero in Taiwan for exerting the island's independence. Nowhere was his determination clearer than in his contact with the Europeans who were attempting to colonize Taiwan.

Cheng's ships frequently skirmished with the well-armed European trading ships. When Cheng heard that the Spanish had

A massive statue of Cheng Ch'eng-kung stands guard over the Chinese port city of Xiamen. Cheng is regarded as a hero for thwarting European efforts to colonize Taiwan.

massacred the Chinese population in the Philippines, he unleashed his fury on the closest Europeans at hand: the Dutch. With an army of thirty thousand soldiers, in 1660 Cheng besieged Fort Zeelandia, the colonial headquarters of the Dutch East India Company, in what is today the city of Tainan in southern Taiwan. His ships circled the bay nearby and fought off attempts to relieve the fort. After two years of siege, the Dutch withdrew from the island altogether, ending European attempts to colonize Taiwan.

China Expands into Taiwan

Cheng's defeat of the Dutch and his establishment of a government ruled locally gave Taiwan its first truly independent state. The government established by Cheng is cited today by independence advocates on Taiwan as a precedent for an independent Taiwan, and Cheng is considered a national hero. However, Cheng's role in Taiwan's history is much more complicated. He was a staunch supporter of the Ming dynasty and intended, if possible, to restore the old dynasty and reunite Taiwan with

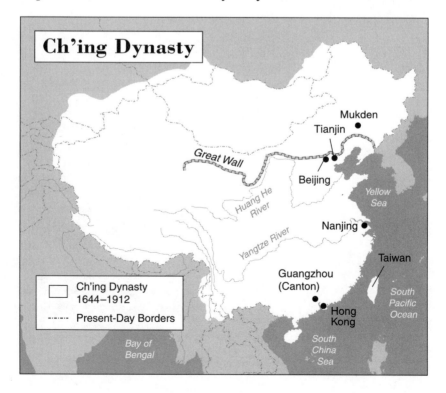

China. Cheng modeled his government on the government of the defeated Ming emperors. He encouraged the cultivation of traditional Chinese arts, such as calligraphy and pottery making, and encouraged the study of classic works of Chinese literature and philosophy that formed the curriculum of those who wanted to hold government positions in China.

When Cheng died in 1663 at the age of thirty-eight, his son, Cheng Ching, inherited his father's fiefdom after fending off a rival claim by his uncle. The third ruler in the pirate dynasty, Cheng Ching attempted to expand his power across the Taiwan Strait to the mainland Chinese province of Fujian. The Ch'ing imperial government decided to put an end to what it considered an attack on China by a family of pirates, and it dispatched an imperial fleet that destroyed Cheng Ching's ships at the Pescadores. The Ch'ing had by that time consolidated its power and presented a formidable military threat. When Ch'ing imperial troops arrived in Taiwan, the people submitted, and Taiwan was formally taken into the Chinese Empire in 1683.

For the first time in its history, Taiwan was officially part of the country that had provided the majority of its immigrants. For most people on Taiwan, however, not much changed. The Chinese were content to have ended the threat posed by Cheng's navy and to have added Taiwan to their enormous empire. Taiwan afterward was largely neglected by the Ch'ing emperors. For the mandarins (public officials) dispatched to rule the various parts of the empire, appointment to Taiwan, considered an unimportant backwater, was extremely undesirable. As a consequence, Ch'ing officials in Taiwan often whiled away their time getting rich through corruption and in some cases smoking opium to relieve their boredom.

A Canadian missionary, George Leslie MacKay, recorded the degenerate state of government in Taiwan during the nineteenth century:

The income attached to any of the offices is not sufficient to support the retinue which must be maintained. As a result there is universal official corruption. From the highest to the lowest, every Chinese official in Formosa has an "itching palm," and the exercise of official functions is always corrupted by the money bribes. The mandarin supplements his income by "squeezing" his attendants and every man and woman who come within his grasp. His attendants have the privilege of recouping themselves by "squeezing" all who through them seek favors from the mandarin. In the matter of bribing and boodling the Chinese official in Formosa could give points to the most accomplished office-seekers and money-grabbers in Washington and Ottawa.[3]

The Ch'ing court's general lack of interest in Taiwan had two significant results. The lax administration and heavy taxation led the population in Taiwan to resent Chinese rule. At the same time, it allowed them to go about their business relatively unhindered, with the exception, of course, of a visit from the hated tax collector.

Although Chinese immigration increased dramatically during China's rule of Taiwan, emigrants sailing from China to Taiwan often resented rule by the Ch'ing court. The Ch'ing government was growing weaker and more corrupt during the nineteenth century, and the administration of Taiwan worsened. Revolts broke out sporadically, threatening to drive the corrupt Ch'ing administrators off the island.

The Ch'ing government was not only weakening in Taiwan but also all over the empire. Europeans who had wrested a number of treaties from the Chinese controlled significant ports on the Chinese coast. The Ch'ing court was in the process of adopting Western methods of warfare and making political reforms to prop up its crumbling empire, but corruption, bureaucratic indifference, and conservative voices that opposed modernization stalled the process. In the meantime another power in Asia, Japan, raced forward with a vigorous modernization program.

Having seen the military power of the Western navies operating in Asia, the Japanese reformed their own military. So successful were they that by the close of the nineteenth century, they had joined the Western powers in claiming rights in China and

This painting depicts the victory of Japanese troops over the Chinese army during the war of 1894–1895.

participating in the carving up of the dying Ch'ing empire. As the Japanese expanded into Chinese-controlled territory, the Ch'ing armies tried to stop them. In 1894, war broke out in Korea, a vassal state of China. The Chinese, who had always considered the Japanese a weak island nation, were soundly defeated by Japanese troops using modern military techniques. It was a rude awakening for the Ch'ing, who watched their empire crumble around them.

The war was formally settled by the Treaty of Shimonoseki, signed in 1895. In accordance with the treaty, the Chinese ceded not only Korea but also Taiwan and the Pescadores to the Japanese. Taiwan, which existed on the fringe of the Chinese Empire, was now lost to the Ch'ing. The implications for the people of Taiwan were enormous.

Under the Rising Sun

In ruling Taiwan, the Japanese Empire's first colony, the Japanese attempted to sever all cultural connections between Taiwan and China. When they raised their national standard, the Rising Sun, above their colonial capital of Taipei, they signaled the beginning of the Japanization of the Taiwanese population.

The Taiwanese responded with defiance. Armed resistance fighters attacked Japanese troops and appealed to China for assistance, but China was too weak to help. The Japanese crushed the Taiwanese resistance movement with their well-trained troops. The Japanese ruled with harsh laws and often punished offenders with beheading. At the same time, they attempted to transform the people of Taiwan into Japanese citizens. The Taiwanese were required to speak Japanese, wear Japanese-style clothing, and proclaim their allegiance to the emperor of Japan. The Japanese also cut off all immigration from China and attempted to stamp out Chinese ways of life on the island.

To instill in the Taiwanese a Japanese-centered outlook, the Japanese built schools and universities where students were required to speak Japanese and learn Japanese history. Japanese

Harvesting Taiwan's Natural Resources

During their fifty-year occupation of Taiwan, the Japanese rapidly modernized many aspects of Taiwan's economy. To ensure that colonization profited the motherland, the Japanese implemented infrastructure projects to increase crop output. They built dams, reservoirs, and aqueducts to help water farmland. As a result, arable land for rice cultivation increased 74 percent, and the land allotted for sugarcane planting increased by 500 percent. Taiwan became a major exporter of rice, sugar, and many fruits and vegetables. Meanwhile, hydroelectric dams provided energy for the manufacture of aluminum, steel, and chemicals.

To reach the riches of the inland mountains, the Japanese constructed mountain cog trains that could climb remarkably steep slopes and blasted tunnels through the mountains to lay tracks for the railway. In total, the Japanese constructed 2,857 miles of railway lines.

The lion's share of the increased production was shipped back to Japan, where it was used to help sustain Japan's military. Although the Japanese siphoned off the newly created wealth, many of the Japanese infrastructure projects, such as road construction and the laying of rail lines, benefited the Taiwanese economy long after the Japanese had departed.

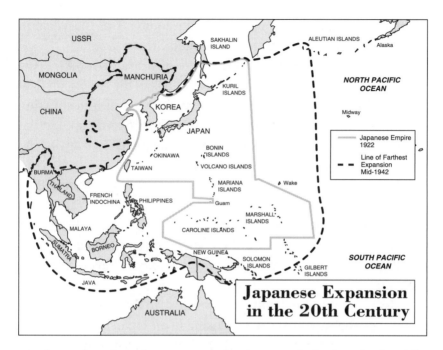

Japanese Expansion in the 20th Century

teachers also placed a great emphasis on technical and scientific subjects, such as forestry, engineering, chemistry, and botany, which could help cultivate industries that would be useful to Japan.

Taiwan quickly took on the appearance of Japan. The colonial governor built his office in Taipei in a style popular among the Japanese at the time. Japanese-style houses replaced Chinese-style architecture. Certain Japanese customs, such as frequent bathing and the removal of shoes when entering a house, were imported, and many are still carried on in Taiwan today.

In the fifty years of Japanese rule, Taiwan experienced tremendous industrial and agricultural growth. New rice strains increased the rice harvests. Camphor was harvested in the central mountains and exported to Japan and other countries. Coal, steel, and other raw materials for industry were all exploited. Even crafts, such as the making of lacquerware, boomed as a result of the demand in Japan.

Much of this new prosperity, however, was diverted to Japan, which was continuing along its expansionist policy. As the Japanese Empire expanded throughout Asia in the early part of the twentieth century, it ran up against the interests of the Western powers: France, Britain, and the United States.

By 1940 the armies of Japan were at war all over Asia. On December 7, 1941, the Japanese navy attacked the American fleet anchored at Pearl Harbor, Hawaii, leaving most of it in smoking ruin or sinking to the bottom of the harbor. The attack led the United States into World War II, a war that would once again lead to a change in government for Taiwan.

During World War II the Japanese squeezed everything they could get out of Taiwan to support their war effort. Taiwanese were even drafted into the Japanese army and made to fight their kin in China. Others seized the chance to resist Japanese rule, hoping a Japanese defeat in the war would end Japanese rule in Taiwan.

By 1944 the Allied powers were close to defeating Nazi Germany, and the Americans were closing in on Japan through a campaign of island hopping through the Pacific. Taiwan was considered as a possible base from which to launch an Allied assault on the Japanese home islands, and Allied bombers attacked Japanese positions on Taiwan. The Allies later bypassed Taiwan and assaulted Okinawa, Japan. With the dropping of atomic bombs on the Japanese cities of Hiroshima and Nagasaki, the Japanese emperor agreed to an unconditional surrender. The Rising Sun flag was lowered in Taiwan, and a new flag, that of Nationalist China, was raised in its place. The date of Taiwan's return to Chinese rule, October 2, is celebrated in Taiwan as Retrocession Day. This holiday, although still officially commemorated, has grown less popular in recent years as the new government has tried to localize Taiwanese identity by downplaying holidays that connect the island to the mother culture in mainland China.

A Republic in Exile 2

While Taiwan was under the rule of imperial Japan, two revolutions erupted in mainland China. Both would have far-reaching consequences for Taiwan. The first was the Nationalist revolution of 1911, which toppled the Ch'ing dynasty and led to the establishment the following year of the Republic of China (ROC), the first republic in Chinese history. The second was the Communist rebellion that destabilized the Nationalist government and eventually led to the civil war between the Communists and Nationalists. The Chinese Civil War, which has never officially ended, resulted in the Nationalist government retreating to the island of Taiwan in 1949. Taiwan became the provisional home of the government of all of China, according to the Nationalists' point of view.

Taiwan today is still officially known as the Republic of China, though most people refer to it by the name Taiwan. Since the Nationalist government retreated to Taiwan, Taiwan has been a republic in exile. The government longed to return to the mainland and reestablish control over all of China. The presence of the Republic of China government in Taiwan and the desire of the Communists in Beijing to recapture Taiwan have largely shaped Taiwan's history since 1949. And the question of what kind of relationship Taiwan should have with China still bedevils the island.

The Founding of the Republic of China

When revolution broke out in 1911 in Wuchang, the provincial capital of China's Hubei province, Chinese revolutionaries holding many different political views united to overthrow the Ch'ing government, the last dynasty of China. For centuries, revolts had dethroned emperors, but each time the uprisings had led only to a change of dynasty. The revolution of 1911, however, removed the last emperor from the throne, ending the Chinese dynastic system, which had survived for thousands of years. The toppling of the Ch'ing dynasty, which put an end to rule by the Manchus, considered an alien people, was almost universally celebrated in China and marked the beginning of a grand political experiment in the world's most populous country.

The victorious revolutionaries formed a new government with a constitution and a provisional president, Sun Yat-sen, who was to rule until national elections could be held. As the head of the new Nationalist government, Sun established a capital at Nanjing on the Yangtze River. Sun's government was based on Western democracies and his own "Three Principles of the People": nationalism, democracy, and the people's well-being. Sun's political ideas were a radical shift from the traditional hierarchy of the Chinese bureaucracy, under which the emperor acted as the father of the nation and was considered a god on Earth. Sun wanted to rid China of its old ways. The Nationalist government, for example, outlawed the practice of foot binding, which left women crippled for life. He wanted the Chinese people to give their allegiance to the nation as opposed to their family or clan. He also wanted people to take part in their own governments through democracy and to raise their standard of living. In Sun's republic, the poor were to become as important as the rich through their use of the vote.

Sun had triumphed in his revolution against the Ch'ing emperor, but forming a government in a country unused to mass political participation proved more difficult. The government at Nanjing in reality ruled only parts of China, mostly in the south. In the north, private armies loyal to regional warlords controlled vast stretches of territory. Sun tried to bring them into the new system of government peacefully, but the warlords were loath to give up their power. As a compromise, Sun abdicated, effectively placing democratic reforms on hold to help ensure stability and unity. The Nationalists voted to hand the presidency to Yuan Shih-k'ai, a powerful military figure during the Ch'ing dynasty. A few months later, Yuan proclaimed himself emperor in Beijing, the

Sun Yat-sen

Sun Yat-sen is one of the towering figures of modern Chinese history. He was one of the chief revolutionaries who advocated the overthrow of the Ch'ing dynasty and is regarded as the founding father of the Republic of China.

Sun was born in 1866 in Guangdong (Canton) province but eventually found his way to Hawaii, where he had relatives. Sun was an ardent student of Chinese history and Western politics. He attended college in Hawaii and later earned a medical degree in Hong Kong. Sun was greatly influenced by both Western democratic systems of government and by the ideologies, such as socialism and communism, that gave rise to revolutions in Russia and elsewhere.

In 1894 Sun organized the Society for Regenerating China in Honolulu, Hawaii, to fight against the Ch'ing government and establish a republic in China. He traveled to overseas communities around the globe, drumming up support and raising funds. In 1911 an uprising broke out in Wuchang, Hubei province. The uprising sparked a national revolt against the Ch'ing government and led to the founding of the Republic of China.

Sun Yat-sen is regarded as the founding father of the Republic of China.

Sun was elected the provisional president of the new republic, but he spent most of his remaining years trying to unite the various warring factions throughout China and lay a foundation for the new government. Sun's Nationalist Party, which grew out of the Society for Regenerating China, was an umbrella organization sheltering revolutionaries of different political ideologies. After his death in 1925, the Communist faction of the Nationalist Party broke away from the party, which was under the leadership of Chiang Kai-shek and the military. The breadth of Sun's political vision is evident in the fact that he is honored as a hero of the state in both the People's Republic of China and the Republic of China on Taiwan.

old capital of the Ch'ing dynasty in the north of China. Yuan's attempt to found a new dynasty enflamed revolutionaries of all stripes and further divided the country.

The Chinese Communist Party

Sun and the Nationalists moved southward to Canton, where they set up a rival government to carry forward democratic government in China. Among the groups struggling to transform Chinese society into a new political entity was the Chinese Communist Party, formed in Shanghai in 1920. Like Sun's ideology, communism had been taken from foreign political theory and had been adapted to fit Chinese society.

The Communists looked to Russia for an example of a successful revolution. In 1917 the Bolsheviks had overthrown Russia's emperor, known as the czar. The new Communist government organized the nation into a series of soviets, or semi-independent units, and founded a new country, the Union of Soviet Socialist Republics (USSR). The Russian Revolution, however, focused on rapid industrial development and gave the urban worker the central role in the new state. In contrast, in China the Chinese Communist Party, under the leadership of party chairman Mao Tsetung, believed that China could rely on the peasantry to carry out the revolution because it was largely an agrarian society. Chinese peasants, who had never taken part in the political life of the country, responded favorably to the Communists, who promised them a better life and an end to the heavy taxes levied by the central government.

The Chinese Communist Party allied itself with other revolutionaries in China, though they had differing political views. The Communists looked favorably on Sun Yat-sen, for example, and joined his Nationalist government in Canton. The government in Canton became an umbrella organization that tried to unite the many factions of Chinese revolutionaries. In the Nationalist Party government, the political spectrum ranged from Communist members on one end to the militarists, landowners, and bankers who had funded the Nationalist revolution. Although the Nationalists wanted to transform Chinese society, they also wanted to protect their privileges. Sun held this uneasy coalition together until his death in 1925, when Chiang Kai-shek inherited the leadership of the Nationalists.

Chiang hailed from the small town of Hsikou in the coastal province of Zhejiang, not far from the great port city of Shanghai. He first made a name for himself in the hurly-burly world of that great metropolis. Shanghai's port and its customs house were at that time controlled by Western powers, notably Britain, France, and the United States. The city was divided into three different concessions: the international concession (primarily British

Chiang Kai-shek was a powerful Nationalist leader. This photo shows him as the commander in chief of the Chinese army, upon his horse, Black Dragon.

The Young Marshall and the Generalissimo

After the overthrow of the Ch'ing dynasty in 1911, while the Nationalist government was still trying to unify the country, a group of fiercely independent warlords exercised control over various parts of northern China. Some were simply bandits, and some were fascinatingly colorful figures, such as Feng Yu-hsiang, known as the Christian General. Feng baptized his troops with a hose, taught them to read, and forbade opium smoking.

One of those warlords played a pivotal role in modern Chinese history: Zhang Xueliang, known as the Young Marshall. Zhang was a Manchurian warlord operating in northern China after being driven from Manchuria by the Japanese. Zhang's father, who had also been a famous warlord, known as the Tiger of Manchuria, was blown up by the Japanese Kwangtung army operating in Manchuria during the 1930s. The death of his father and the loss of their ancestral fiefdom instilled in the Young Marshall a desire for revenge and a determination to defeat the Japanese.

During the 1930s the Japanese were moving southward from Manchuria along the coast of eastern China. The Chinese were divided, fighting a civil war between the Communists and the Nationalists. The Young Marshall, although not a Communist, believed that only through a united front between the Communists and Nationalists could the Chinese drive out the Japanese. To forge an alliance, the Young Marshall secured a meeting with Generalissimo Chiang Kai-shek, the Nationalist leader, at the city of Xi'an. When the generalissimo arrived in Xi'an, he found himself the prisoner of the Young Marshall and was released only after he agreed to join the Communists in fighting the Japanese. The event, known today as the Xi'an Incident, created an alliance between the Communists and Nationalists to fight the Japanese.

As part of the bargain to form a united front, the Young Marshall had surrendered himself to Chiang Kai-shek, and he remained a prisoner of the Nationalists for most of his life. Even after the Nationalists retreated to Taiwan, the Young Marshall lived under a loose house arrest. On Sundays he attended the same church as the generalissimo and became good friends with his son, Chiang Ching-kuo. After the Young Marshall's house arrest was finally lifted in the 1980s, the Manchurian warlord moved to Hawaii, where he died in 2001.

and American, where the customs house was located); the Chinese concession, which provided most of the city's laborers, or coolies as they were called; and the French concession.

In Shanghai, Chiang Kai-shek joined the Green Gangs, which operated largely in the French concession, where their members were elected to local governing bodies. Shanghai was ruled by foreign powers, who had wrested a number of cities from the ailing Ch'ing dynasty by treaty after the Opium Wars of the mid-nineteenth century. These cities were known as "treaty ports," and Chinese government troops were forbidden from entering. Because of this, the Green Gangs operated with some degree of immunity. They controlled the opium market, gambling, brothels, and many legitimate aspects of the city's commercial life.

By joining the Green Gangs, Chiang won many powerful friends who helped advance his career. Many of these friends also backed the 1911 revolution against the Ch'ing dynasty. Because of Chiang's supreme self-confidence and his familiarity with military tactics, Sun selected him as his right-hand man. When the government moved to Canton, Chiang became the leader of the Whampoa Military Academy, which raised the Nationalist army to protect the new republic. After Sun's death in 1925, Chiang became the head of the Nationalist government and struggled, as generalissimo (supreme general) of the Nationalist army, to pacify China by launching expeditions against the warlords in the north.

The Chinese Civil War

The Communists reacted to Chiang's leadership with trepidation. As head of the military and with close connections to rich bankers and landowners, Chiang represented everything the Communists were fighting against. A rift in the Nationalist Party seemed certain to open.

In 1927 Chiang struck in Shanghai. Using Green Gang members and Nationalist agents, he closed down trade unions and leftist newspapers and killed Communists throughout the city. Days of killing followed, and the Communists were driven out of the city. Two of the most important leaders of the Communist Party were in Shanghai at that time. Mao Tse-tung, future chairman and national leader of the People's Republic of China, and Chou En-lai, who would later serve as premier, narrowly escaped the death squads. Mao and Chou would never trust the generalissimo again, and their determination to transform China into a Communist state only hardened.

Although Chiang's purge of the Communists in Shanghai had succeeded in ridding the city of its leftist influences, it had also given the Communists good propaganda to use against the generalissimo, who they claimed was only interested in making himself supreme in China and cared not at all for the welfare of the people.

The incident marked the beginning of the Chinese Civil War, fought between the Communists and the Nationalists off and on until 1949. The Civil War was interrupted only by World War II, during which Japan invaded and occupied most of eastern China. Driven from the Nationalist capital of Nanjing by the Japanese, Chiang set up a provisional capital at Chongqing on the upper reaches of the Yangtze River in southwestern China. His troops were supplied by Allied aircraft flying food and weapons over the Himalayas and by Allied fighters, including a volunteer group known as the Flying Tigers, under the command of an American named Claire Chennault. For some time, the Allies thought they could open a land front against the Japanese in China, but they were repeatedly frustrated by Chiang's reluctance to fight the Japanese.

Chiang was clearly more concerned with ridding the country of Communists, whom the Nationalists referred to as "red bandits," while the Allies defeated the Japanese in the Pacific campaign. Allied commanders repeatedly pleaded with Chiang to join forces with the Communists, who were waging guerrilla warfare against the Japanese in northern China from their remote base at Yan'an.

The Nationalists at various times did form an alliance with the Communists and fought the Japanese ostensibly in a "united front." The Nationalist forces and Communist forces settled on different areas of operation in their fight against the Japanese. But when Nationalist and Communist troops ran across each other, they often fought each other. Moreover, Chiang was using much of the American aid (both weapons and money) to launch campaigns against the Communists, leaving the Allied forces to fight the Japanese.

When the Japanese surrendered in 1945, the civil war broke out with renewed intensity. The Communists controlled large parts of the countryside and the Nationalists many of the coastal cities. To fight the Communists, Chiang resorted to forced conscription of Chinese peasants, who bitterly resented such treatment. By

Defeated by the Communist army, Nationalist troops march out of the province of Canton in 1949.

1949 the Communists had driven the Nationalists into an ever-shrinking area of China. The Communist army, known as the People's Liberation Army, gained new recruits daily, while the Nationalist army withered. Fearing complete destruction, the Nationalist government retreated to Taiwan in a massive convoy of ships carrying not only the remnants of the Nationalist army but also government members, industrial equipment, the national treasury, the reserves of China's banks, the imperial art collection, and approximately 1.5 million mainland Chinese, known afterward in Taiwan as the "mainlanders."

The Nationalists in Taiwan

On arriving in Taiwan, the Nationalist government, also known as the Kuomintang, named Taipei the provisional capital of the Republic of China (ROC). It was meant to serve as a temporary refuge for the Nationalist armies to regroup before retaking the mainland. The government built temporary houses for its soldiers, established military bases, and ruled Taiwan at a temporary campaign headquarters.

Chiang in effect imported the entire Nationalist government to Taiwan, where he ruled as chief executive from the old Japanese governor's office in Taipei. The government consisted of the executive office, or Executive Yuan, the Judicial Yuan, and the Legislative Yuan. The functions of the three branches resembled those of the executive, judicial, and legislative branches of the American government. They were designed to diffuse power, preventing any one branch or person from becoming supreme.

In addition to the three branches, the ROC constitution established two particularly Chinese branches of government: the Examination Yuan and the Control Yuan. The first was designed to administer tests for civil servants. Its inclusion among the five branches of government indicated the high value that the Chinese traditionally placed on education and its importance to the Chinese bureaucracy. Chinese scholars were encouraged to be poets and calligraphers, but they were also expected to administer the country. The Control Yuan, on the other hand, had evolved from

the censorate in the traditional Chinese bureaucracy that monitored the moral behavior of imperial officials. The Control Yuan
was intended to watch the branches of government for abuses of
power and investigate specific government members if they were
accused of improper or illegal behavior.

The Nationalist government also tried to stamp a Chinese character on its new capital in Taiwan, renaming the streets around the
government offices and throughout Taipei. Streets with names such
as Beiping, the Nationalist name for Beijing, Nanking, named
after the Nationalist capital, and Chongqing, named for the wartime
capital, served for the mainlanders as reminders of home.

Martial Law

While the government was still on the mainland, Chiang had sus-
pended the constitution and declared martial law, allowing him
to harness the resources of the government to fight the Communists and limit dissent. In Taiwan, martial law was also imposed.
Despite the democratic structure of the government, all branches
took their orders from Chiang, who ruled with dictatorial powers. In other words, Chiang put off Sun's dream of establishing
a democracy for the Chinese people. This had drastic implications for the people living on Taiwan after the arrival of the Nationalists.

When Chiang arrived in Taiwan in 1949, relations between
the Nationalist military government that had arrived in 1945
when the Japanese departed, and the local population, had already deteriorated to an alarming state. Revolt had broken out
once in 1947 and was ruthlessly stamped out by the Nationalist commander general Chen Yi. Since that time, Chen Yi had
relied on Nationalist troops and a network of secret police to
keep the local population in hand. Nationalist prisons bulged
with local citizens who were deemed political dissidents, and
executions were common.

Realizing that further unrest on Taiwan could tie up his troops
on the island and undermine his plans to reinvade China, Chiang set about trying to improve relations with the local population. In a symbolic act, he ordered the execution of Chen Yi

and heaped the blame for bad relations on the disgraced general. Chiang also accepted local Taiwanese into the ranks of the Nationalist army and recruited locals for government positions.

Chiang's gestures helped calm the situation, but they were largely superficial. The mainlanders who had arrived with Chiang reserved most of the high government and military posts for themselves and received preferential treatment in many professions. The discrimination, however, cut both ways. Local Taiwanese often refused jobs to the thousands of unemployed and aging soldiers who arrived with Chiang. Many of these old soldiers were peasants from the mainland recruited to fight the Communists. In Taiwan, they found themselves cut off from their families in a strange land with few skills and often no education. These mainlanders, far less visible than the government elite and their wealthy backers who formed the top stratum of society, often eked out a miserable existence. To take care of them, the Nationalists built public housing and distributed pensions.

Their more privileged compatriots in the government, meanwhile, continued to rule Taiwan as if they were in China. The Legislative Yuan, for example, was composed almost exclusively of representatives elected on the mainland. They were separated from their constituents and their constituencies but continued in their government positions with all the privileges they afforded.

To enforce the idea that they represented all of China, the Nationalists required that Mandarin, a northern dialect of Chinese adopted as the official language by the Nationalist government while it was still in China, be used in all government posts, schools, the military, and all other public aspects of life. The problem for the Taiwanese was that after fifty years of Japanese rule, under which they were required to speak Japanese, few of them spoke Mandarin, a dialect native to Beijing and the surrounding areas. At home, they spoke the Taiwanese dialect of Chinese, known both as Minan hua (the dialect of the area of the Fujian province south of the Min River) and Taiwanese. The imposition of Mandarin created a linguistic barrier, impeding local Taiwanese from securing choice positions in many aspects of society and creating much tension among the locals.

The February 28 Incident

In 1947, while civil war between the Communists and Nationalists still raged on mainland China, Taiwan was ruled by Nationalist forces under the command of General Chen Yi. Tension ran high between the Nationalist troops sent to administer the island and the local population, which resented what they considered high-handed treatment by the newly arrived government.

On the night of February 28, plainclothes policemen attempted to arrest a woman selling cigarettes on the black market, in violation of the government's monopoly on alcohol and tobacco products. As the policemen struggled with the woman, an angry crowd began to harass the police. When the police fired into the crowd, a riot broke out. Over the next few days it spread across the island. Violence between Taiwanese and mainland troops continued until the end of March. Both sides committed savage acts of cruelty and murdered innocent people. As many as twenty thousand people died before order was restored on the island by Nationalist troops.

The incident, later known as the February 28 Incident, has been a lasting source of tension between the two main groups of Chinese people on Taiwan: those who came before 1945 and those who came after. Today, a peace park in Taipei houses a small museum that commemorates the tragic incident.

Increasing tension was the attitude of Nationalist officials such as General Chen Yi, the governor of Taiwan from 1945 to 1949. Although he was fluent in both Taiwanese and Japanese, Chen spoke only in Mandarin while he was in Taiwan. The Nationalists' use of Mandarin and discouragement of the local dialects caused a division between the newly arrived Chinese and the earlier immigrants. And even today a local Taiwanese who speaks Mandarin with a heavy Taiwanese accent is often looked down upon.

As they re-sinicized the local population, the Nationalists also eliminated Japanese influences still lingering in Taiwanese society. In classrooms where the Taiwanese were once forced to celebrate the glories of the Japanese emperors, they now were required to study Chinese civilization, generally under a portrait of Chiang Kai-shek, which adorned almost all public places.

Nowhere was the emphasis on a China-centric curriculum stronger than in the requirements for civil servants. Civil service exams required a detailed understanding of the Chinese classics, mainland geography, thousands of years of imperial history, and, of course, the history of the Republic of China. The tests, strictly regulated by the Examination Yuan, ensured that those entering the government would have the background to continue their posts once the Nationalists returned to China.

A soldier walks his bicycle past a poster of Chiang Kai-shek that urges the people of Taiwan to train their bodies and strengthen their patriotic spirit.

Other organs of the government also spread Nationalist propaganda. The Government Information Office, a bureau under the Executive Yuan, for example, could close newspapers and radio stations and censor publications, broadcasts, and even films. A foreign correspondent writing in 1967, when Taiwan was still under martial law, wrote,

> Cinema censorship might be bad or annoying but it's got to be severe to top Taiwan's.
>
> The foreign resident and the Chinese think the censor has so much uninhibited scissor-wielding power in Taipei, island stronghold of the Nationalist Chinese, that some have sworn off films altogether. Others will only venture into a movie house after first having been assured by friends that the film is understandable.
>
> One out of every three films imported or made on Taiwan is either banned completely or, what's even worse, cut beyond all understanding. [4]

What the Nationalists did not like they censored, and at the same time they promoted their own messages through state-owned media. The government of the Republic of China believed that it was fighting for its very existence. It lingered in exile in Taiwan while dreaming of a return to the mainland. The country constantly prepared for war with the Chinese Communists. At the same time, Chiang Kai-shek kept good relations with the Western democracies, promoting himself both as an anti-Communist fighter and as a democratic alternative to the Communist People's Republic of China.

The Other China

3

In the years after the founding of the People's Republic of China in 1949, the Republic of China on Taiwan existed in the official diplomacy of many of the Western democracies as the true representative of the Chinese people, though its influence was limited to the island of Taiwan and a few smaller nearby islets. Taiwan became "the other China" and was raised to an unprecedented level of importance on the world stage.

The island that had been at various times a minor port for European ships engaged in the China trade, a lawless land on the edge of the Chinese Empire, and a small Japanese colony, found itself at the center of world attention and was included in the decision-making processes of world powers.

The reason for Taiwan's sudden rise in visibility was the fact that most Western countries refused to recognize the Communist government in Beijing. When, in 1949, Mao Tse-tung, chairman of the Chinese Communist Party, stood in Beijing's Tiananmen Square and proclaimed the founding of the People's Republic of China, the Western powers described it as the "fall" of China. In his speech, Mao triumphantly announced that China had stood up, ending more than a hundred years of decline under the Ch'ing and repudiating the unequal treaties that had ceded the sovereignty of China's most important port cities to Western control. The Western powers, and especially the United States, turned their attention to Chiang Kai-shek, as the president of the Republic of China, whom they hoped would eventually retake the mainland and rid it of communism.

The Cold War in the East

After the "fall" of China to communism, Western democracies supported Taiwan as an ally in the fierce ideological battle known as the Cold War, which had broken out after World War II. The war had ended the threats posed by Germany, Japan, and their allies, but as soon as the Allied powers marched into Berlin in the European theater of war, they started quarreling. The Allied powers had always been a mismatched group of nations with incompatible political visions of government. Democracies waged

Mao Tse-tung proclaims the founding of the People's Republic of China at Tiananmen Square on October 1, 1949.

Quemoy's Flying Bomb Cutlery

The island of Quemoy, known locally as Jinmen, must rank as one of the most heavily shelled spots on Earth. Lying just off the coast of the Chinese city of Amoy, in the mainland province of Fujian, Quemoy was held by the Nationalists when they retreated to Taiwan in 1949. The tiny island was considered as a possible stepping-stone for an invasion of the mainland. Because of its possible use as a frontline staging ground, the Nationalists fortified Quemoy and the nearby island of Matsu with one-third of the Nationalist army.

The proximity of Quemoy to the Chinese mainland made it a tempting target for the People's Republic of China. In 1950 the People's Liberation Army (PLA) launched its first artillery barrage of the island. It then made an unsuccessful attempt to capture the Nationalist stronghold. In 1954 China's leader, Mao Tse-tung, ordered his troops to try again, but the U.S. Seventh Fleet sailed into the Taiwan Strait, foiling the plan. To prevent further Communist advances, the United States soon after took Quemoy into its defense perimeter.

Despite the pledge of the Americans to protect Quemoy, Mao tried to capture the island one last time in 1958. To weaken the island's defenses, the PLA shore batteries fired fifty thousand shells at the island. The U.S. Navy again appeared in the Taiwan Strait, and the Chinese backed down. The United States also rushed howitzers to the island, capable of firing nuclear shells to wipe out the Communist shore batteries, but it never supplied the shells. From 1958 until 1979, when the United States officially recognized the People's Republic of China, the Communists limited the shelling to alternate days, allowing for the return of some normalcy for the people of the island.

In later years, only about fifty to one hundred shells dropped onto the island each day before the attacks stopped altogether. Many of the shells carried propaganda instead of explosives, but they nonetheless caused damage to local houses and occasionally caused injury or death. The shelling and the constant threat of war prevented Quemoy from developing normal economic enterprises, but the people of Quemoy found a profitable use for the millions of shells that lay about the island. They worked the metal of the shell casings into knives, which became known as "flying bomb knives" and became a common item in Taiwanese kitchens.

war alongside Communist dictatorships. Many believed that the wartime cooperation of the Soviet Union and the United States, the two largest of the Allied nations, would not outlast the war. The tensions that developed between the two countries after the war confirmed the suspicions.

After World War II ended, the Soviets retained control over the countries of Eastern Europe that they had liberated from the grip of the Nazis, and they planted pro-Soviet Communist regimes throughout the region. The Americans, British, French, and other democratic powers believed that they must prevent communism from spreading. The United States and the Soviet Union emerged as the chief antagonists in what became the Cold War.

It was against this backdrop that the news of the "fall" of China was received. The Americans and their allies watched in horror as the world's most populous country, China, joined the world's largest country, the Soviet Union, under the umbrella of international communism. In the Cold War terminology of the time, the Republic of China on Taiwan was called "Free China."

British prime minister Winston Churchill had described the Soviet Union and its satellite nations as the land behind the iron curtain, impenetrable and menacing. Adapting the terminology to the Asian situation, Communist China was described as the land behind the bamboo curtain. Taiwan gave the Western democracies a platform from which to pierce the bamboo curtain should war break out in the Far East. As a result, the United States flooded Taiwan with weapons and money to ensure the viability of its ally, and both sides of the Taiwan Strait built up their armed forces as quickly as possible for a showdown.

Nowhere was the situation more dangerous than on the tiny islands of Quemoy, known locally as Jinmen, and Matsu. The islets off the coast of China's Fujian province were under the control of Nationalist forces. From the early days of the Nationalist retreat to Taiwan, the ROC government heavily fortified the islands, largely with American-supplied weapons, to serve as forward observation posts to provide early warning in case of an attack by the Communists or as a forward base to prepare for the retaking of the mainland.

In 1950 Mao Tse-tung had consolidated his power on the mainland and turned his attention to his enemies on Taiwan. His first targets were Quemoy and Matsu, visible from the mainland and a lasting reminder that the civil war was unresolved. He unleashed fierce artillery barrages against the tiny islands to weaken Nationalist positions for an invasion of China. Following the bombardment, Mao dispatched amphibious landing craft to retake Quemoy. The People's Liberation Army (PLA) met with fierce resistance from the Nationalist troops. The Communist forces suffered twenty-three thousand casualties, and another seven thousand PLA soldiers were captured. The failure to capture Quemoy dashed Mao's hope for a quick invasion of Taiwan.

The successful defense of Quemoy showed that Taiwan could be counted on to help the United States contain Communist China. It strengthened Taiwan's relationship with the United States and convinced the Americans that Taiwan was a valuable ally in the Cold War.

The Korean War

The same year, war erupted on the Korean Peninsula between the Communist North Koreans and the pro-U.S. South Koreans. Korea had been divided at the thirty-eighth parallel with an independent government on each side. In 1950 the north launched an attack across the thirty-eighth parallel in an attempt to reunite the country under a Communist government. To aid in the venture, the Soviets supplied advisers and aircraft, and the Communist Chinese supplied soldiers, officially listed as volunteers.

In invading South Korea, the Communist bloc countries— North Korea, the Soviet Union, and the People's Republic of China—gambled that Western forces would not go to war over a small country in Asia. They lost the bet. The aggression was condemned in the United Nations, and a coalition of forces, under UN mandate, poured into South Korea to stop the Communist forces. General Douglas MacArthur, serving as the chief of the American occupation forces on Japan, led a landing at In'chŏn that helped stem the Communist advance. MacArthur later ordered troops across the border with China, which was supplying

U.S. Marines stand guard over captured Chinese Communists during the Korean War.

troops and soldiers to North Korea. MacArthur's action was unauthorized by the U.S. president, who is the commander in chief of the U.S. armed forces. It triggered a massive counterattack by the People's Liberation Army, which poured across the Korean border, driving UN forces southward. In 1951 President Harry Truman dismissed and publicly reprimanded MacArthur.

The Korean War lasted until 1953, with heavy fighting taking place in the rugged, and often frigid, hills of Korea. When the shooting stopped, the border was restored at the thirty-eighth parallel. Although the war was costly for UN troops, it was considered a victory for the UN because it contained Communist aggression and proved the UN's resolve.

The war had two important consequences for Taiwan. First, it proved that Western democracies were willing to combat Communist forces to protect Asian peoples. This greatly bolstered Taiwan's trust in the United States, which was supplying Taiwan with weapons and signaling that it would assist the Republic of China if it were attacked by the mainland Chinese. This belief was further bolstered by the action of U.S. forces in the Taiwan Strait during the Korean War. At the start of the war, Mao believed that UN-mandated action in Korea would distract the United States long enough for him to launch an invasion of Taiwan. To prevent the invasion, the United States dispatched the U.S. Seventh Fleet, its prime Pacific Fleet, into the Taiwan Strait, successfully warding off a Chinese advance.

A second consequence of the Korean War for Taiwan was the repatriation to Taiwan of prisoners of war in UN hands after the Korean War. These soldiers had originally been captured by the Chinese Communists during the Chinese Civil War and had remained their prisoners. When the fighting broke out in Korea, Mao threw the former Nationalist troops into battle to help the North Korean side. After the war ended, these soldiers chose to be repatriated not to the People's Republic but to the Republic of China on Taiwan, where they received pensions and were treated as heroes. Some of them later joined the Nationalist army on Taiwan and hoped to return to the mainland with an invasion force. Others kept pressure on the government by lobbying for an invasion of the mainland to topple the Communists. They provided a good source of propaganda for Nationalist government and military leaders who wanted to ensure that the government would not veer away from its intention of returning to China.

The Korean War highlighted the dangers posed by mainland China and showed both Taiwan and the United States that the Communist Chinese were willing to send soldiers into battle under certain circumstances. But even though the United States had bolstered support for Taiwan during the Korean War, the likelihood of Nationalist forces launching an invasion to recapture China was diminishing.

Post–Korean War Intrigues

Chiang Kai-shek never gave up the dream of returning to mainland China, but as time went by the goal became increasingly unlikely. With generous support from the Soviet Union, China built up an impressive military and spent heavily on weapons research and the procurement of ever more modern weapons.

The Nationalists were limited to trying to keep up with the Communist Chinese in the cross-strait arms race and conducting occasional raids on the mainland. Raids from Taiwan into the mainland—some employing amphibious landing craft and some using paratroopers—provided good propaganda for the Nationalist Chinese in that they supported their image as staunch anti-Communists. But the raids almost always ended in complete failure, with soldiers either killed or captured and no military objectives achieved.

The United States sometimes encouraged these raids to probe Chinese strength and sometimes discouraged them, fearing that the Chinese would launch counterattacks. To make the situation more confusing, U.S. government agencies often pursued competing policies. The State Department, for example, often pressed for diplomatic solutions and an opening of relations with the Communist government in China. Some advocates of opening relations with China pointed out that the United States carried on diplomatic exchanges with the Soviets and others who had government systems that they opposed.

Members of other U.S. government agencies, on the other hand, wanted to keep pressure on the Chinese Communists and advocated military engagement, sabotage, black propaganda, and other methods to destabilize and undermine Communist China. The Central Intelligence Agency (CIA) built substantial ties with the Nationalist government and military and often encouraged covert activities against China. In his biography of Chiang Ching-kuo, *The Generalissimo's Son,* Jay Taylor, a former member of the U.S. Foreign Service, indicates the extent of CIA involvement with the Nationalists on Taiwan: "As one former [CIA] agency officer recalled, over the course of twenty years since the Korean

War the agency provided to the Nationalists 'a cornucopia of money, arms, equipment, and training.'"[5]

The Cold War helped keep Taiwan in the minds of strategic thinkers in the United States, who believed the island to be extremely important to U.S. foreign policy. Changes in the world

---

The Curious Case of Taiwan-Mongolia Relations

The diplomatic relationship between the Republic of China (ROC) and Mongolia well illustrates the historical baggage of the Nationalist government on Taiwan. Until the year 2002 the ROC government still claimed to be the ruler of all of Nationalist China as it had left it in 1949. Among territories on the old map of the Republic of China, which hung in classrooms and government offices until the late 1990s, was the country of Mongolia—a steppe land nestled between northern China and Russia.

Unwilling to drop the fiction that the Nationalist government maintained rule over the Mongolians, the Nationalists set up an official government office, the Mongolian and Tibetan Affairs Commission, to govern those two provinces that the Republic of China had officially ruled over until 1949. This meant that from Taiwan's point of view, Taipei as the provisional capital of the Republic of China (which still officially claimed Mongolia as its own) was also the provisional capital of Tibet and Mongolia. Yet Mongolia had first claimed independence from China in 1911, after the overthrow of the Ch'ing dynasty. In 1946 the ROC government recognized Mongolia's claim as an independent country along with the rest of the world. The recognition of Mongolia, however, was withdrawn in 1953, and the ROC reasserted the claim that Mongolia belonged to Nationalist China.

Relations lingered in this curious state until 2002, when the ROC government on Taiwan finally dispatched a de facto ambassador to Mongolia and received a diplomatic official from that independent nation. With this gesture, the republic recognized Mongolia as an independent nation for the second time. To further normalize the relationship, the work of the Mongolian and Tibetan Affairs Commission was transferred to the Ministry of Foreign Affairs. Tibet is still a part of the People's Republic of China and so has no official relations with Taiwan, but Mongolian citizens today can receive a visa from the Taiwanese representative office in their capital of Ulaanbaatar to travel to Taipei—the city that for so long claimed to be their provisional capital.

situation, however, caused a sudden reversal of the policy and a tremendous setback for Taiwan's international position.

Knocked Off the World Stage

In the late 1960s relations between the Soviet Union and China deteriorated. Although the two countries both subscribed to a dream of international communism, they had different ideas of what that meant. The Soviets considered themselves the leaders of the international struggle, and the Chinese often bristled at having to play second fiddle. Moreover, by adapting communism to China, Mao had opened an ideological rift with the Soviets. The Soviets, who were no more open to debate with foreign powers than they were open to domestic opposition, deemed Mao's divergence from the Soviet Union's Communist system as a form of heresy.

The Soviets rebuked Mao's independence by withdrawing promises of support and ordering Soviet citizens, including many technical advisers, working in China to return home. This episode, known as "the Sino-Soviet split," delighted the Americans, who watched as the once-monolithic specter of communism broke into its constituent parts. The United States was also at the time fighting a war in Vietnam to protect the South Vietnamese against Chinese-backed Communist North Vietnam and a local Communist insurgency. The war was proceeding miserably, and citizens of the United States wanted to end U.S. involvement.

As U.S. president Richard Nixon watched Sino-Soviet relations crumble, he decided to approach China to see if he could ease tensions and help get the United States out of Vietnam. China was the main source of support for North Vietnam, and Nixon gambled that improving relations with the Chinese might help encourage China to stop its support for North Vietnam, thereby making it easier for the United States to negotiate an end to the war in Vietnam.

To reach an agreement with the Chinese, Nixon dispatched National Security adviser Henry Kissinger to Beijing in 1971 for secret talks with the Chinese. Kissinger found the Chinese receptive to the American overture, and the following year Nixon

Chairman Mao Tse-tung welcomes President Richard Nixon to China in October 1972.

visited China himself and met with China's leader, Mao Tse-tung, and Premier Chou En-lai. The trip proved to be enormously popular with Americans, who were happy to see relations improving. As a result of the warming relations between the two countries, the United States dropped its opposition to China entering the United Nations. Up to that point, the Republic of China (Taiwan) had occupied the China seat at the UN. The UN's acceptance of the People's Republic of China caused Taiwan to withdraw in protest. In an instant, the island government, which had represented all of China on the world stage, found itself out in the cold.

Although the United States had been a close ally of the Nationalist government on Taiwan, the Americans put their own greater strategic concerns over the concerns of the Nationalists. In other words, the United States was willing to improve relations with the Communist Chinese to widen China's split with the Soviets, the chief Cold War adversary of the United States, as Shelley Rigger explains in her book *Politics in Taiwan:*

> In the 1970s, anti-communism still was strong in the US, Taiwan's most important diplomatic partner. But the Cold War justification for supporting Nationalists—walling off communism in Asia—was less persuasive after the Sino-Soviet split. As animosity replaced socialist fraternity in Beijing-Moscow relations, US policy-makers began to consider detente with Beijing. Ideological opposition to communism in all its forms gradually lost ground to *Realpolitik* calculation in which "playing the China card" against the Soviets made good strategic sense.[6]

The "One-China" Principle

The thawing of relations between the United States and Communist China continued over the next decade, and in 1979 U.S. president Jimmy Carter severed official diplomatic ties with the Republic of China (Taiwan) and announced that the United States would recognize the People's Republic of China. After thirty years of refusing to accept China as a Communist country, the United States had abruptly changed course. The news was devastating for the Taiwanese, who went from being the official representative of all of China to a population officially without a country. The Republic of China ceased to exist in the diplomatic world.

In negotiations with Beijing, Carter accepted a political compromise on Taiwan according to which the United States would neither recognize Taiwan as a part of China nor as an independent country. The United States and China agreed to the "one-China" principle, whereby there would officially be only one China. However, the Chinese, Americans, and Taiwanese could each interpret the meaning of the vague term *one China* as their political needs demanded. It was an illogical position that allowed Beijing and Washington to reach an agreement. But the policy left Taiwan without diplomatic recognition. The Taiwanese were free to interpret the one-China principle as meaning that the Republic of China was the sole legitimate government of

Taiwan and the World Health Organization

The difficulties of Taiwan's international standing are illustrated in its struggle to join the World Health Organization (WHO). WHO was established in 1948 by the United Nations. Because disease can spread quickly around the globe and health-related information in one area could be extremely useful in other areas, WHO was created to facilitate health-related information and activities around the world—regardless of politics. According to the WHO constitution, however, membership is limited to sovereign states. Because Taiwan is officially unrecognized as an independent nation by most of the world, it is generally not permitted to participate in international organizations. However, in recent years Taiwan has been lobbying WHO and its member nations to join under "observer status," which would deny Taiwan full membership but allow the nation to participate in health-related activities and the sharing of health-related information. Delegates from Taiwan, who regularly lobby the organization, often point out that the Vatican, the Palestinian Authority, and the International Red Cross have been granted observer status though none of them is a sovereign state.

Among the 192 member states of WHO, China has put up the most resistance to Taiwan's bid to join the health organization. Because China considers Taiwan a renegade province and insists that the one-China principle be recognized uniformly in dealings with Taiwan, the island nation has had an uphill battle to secure WHO participation. Taiwan's lobbying efforts, however, have secured powerful supporters. The European Union, Japan, and a host of other countries have agreed to support Taiwan's entry. In 2003 the U.S. Congress passed a resolution authorizing the State Department to push for Taiwan's bid at the WHO World Health Assembly, where membership questions are determined. Taiwan's efforts to join the WHO, even with limited membership rights, reveal the trouble of being officially unofficial.

U.S. president Jimmy Carter (right) speaks at a press conference with Chinese premier Deng Xiaoping. Carter severed diplomatic ties with Taiwan.

all of China, but few agreed with this interpretation because the ROC controlled only Taiwan and a few nearby islands.

As part of the agreement, Taiwan would not be allowed to declare independence. That suited the Republic of China government, which still wanted to retake the mainland. The United States also demanded that the question of reunification of Taiwan and mainland China be settled peacefully and with the consent of both sides of the Taiwan Strait.

Many in the U.S. government were unhappy with Carter's decision and wanted to make sure the United States did not abandon its Cold War ally. Congress, therefore, responded to the recognition of the People's Republic of China and the severing of official ties with Taiwan by passing in April 1979 the Taiwan Relations Act, the central pillar of American-Taiwanese relations to this day. The passage of the act obligated the United States by law to "provide Taiwan with arms of a defensive character; and to maintain the capacity of the United States to resist any resort to force or other forms of coercion that would jeopardize the security, or the social or economic system, of the people on Taiwan."[7]

As a result, the United States became the de facto protector of Taiwan while at the same time withdrawing official recognition. The American embassy in Taipei closed its doors, and a new organization, the American Institute on Taiwan (AIT), represented U.S. interests on the island. The AIT was officially not considered a consulate, but it was staffed by former State Department diplomats who were asked to hand in their resignations before accepting the post. The new organization went out of its way to look like a private organization so as not to upset Beijing. As it coordinated arms sales and other diplomatic exchanges for the defense of the island, it kept a low profile. This strange situation was described by the first head of the AIT, longtime U.S. diplomat Charles T. Cross:

> We knew from the start that we would encounter determined efforts by the ruling Kuomintang [Nationalist] leadership—indeed everyone on Taiwan—to demonstrate to the world that AIT was "just an embassy by another name" and that its officers were conducting what amounted to official business between governments while pretending they didn't. Therefore, AIT's operating style would determine how well the United States could politely, but firmly, maintain the unofficial look of the working arrangements, thereby observing our agreements with the PRC [People's Republic of China].[8]

Other nations soon opened equally unofficial-sounding organizations to conduct their relations with Taipei. Finding that Republic of China embassies were no longer welcome even in the countries of allies, the Taiwanese changed their embassies in other countries, giving them the innocuous-sounding name of Taipei Economic and Cultural Organization to carry out their own foreign policy.

Since the end of the Chinese Civil War in 1949, Taiwan's fortunes had been on a roller-coaster ride. It was first welcomed into a powerful alliance during the Cold War and then over the next couple of decades it began to slowly lose importance on the international stage. By the late 1970s Taiwan had all but vanished from the world of international diplomacy, nominally recognized as a part of an undefined "one-China," and at the same time as an island with its own independent government.

Economic and Social Transformation

4

As Taiwan's diplomatic visibility plummeted and its embassies and consulates took on bureaucratic-sounding names, its relationships with the rest of the world took different forms. Foreign manufacturers, mostly from the United States, Europe, and Japan, found Taiwan's leaders friendly about business propositions and discovered that Taiwan's cheap labor made the island an attractive place to set up factories. The Taiwanese people responded to the influx of foreign business with remarkable agility, mastering the intricacies of production and slowly opening their own businesses. Foreign investment and a strong entrepreneurial spirit among the Taiwanese led to rapid economic growth rates and a quickly rising standard of living.

As Taiwan earned a reputation as a manufacturer for the world, the Taiwanese, growing richer from the economic successes, began demanding more participation in the political system. From the 1960s to the 1990s, Taiwanese society underwent dramatic economic and social changes. Taiwan, lingering in diplomatic isolation from the rest of the world, became a model for economic growth and started to struggle free from martial law.

The Economic Miracle

Brooking no political dissent, the Nationalists on Taiwan nonetheless adopted some remarkably forward-thinking economic policies that led to a rise in living standards for the people of Taiwan in a remarkably short period of time. The presence of a strong central government, which could set economic policy and carry it out without opposition, proved to be a great benefit for Taiwan's economy. Today the political legacy of the Nationalist Party is hotly debated in Taiwan, but most Taiwanese agree that certain government policies of the period aided Taiwan's quick economic growth and led to a transformation of the Taiwanese economy.

Historically, Taiwan had played different economic roles in the region. First, it had been a regional trading center for Europeans in Taiwan and for Chinese merchants. This early stage of the local economy relied on the island's position in the major sea lanes of East Asia and the supremacy of shipping as a means of transportation.

Under the Japanese, Taiwan's economy advanced considerably for several reasons, becoming Asia's second-leading economy. Japan, whose economy was the largest in Asia, invested heavily in Taiwan's infrastructure, introduced heavy industry, improved access to the natural resources of the interior through the construction of highways and railroads, introduced new strains of rice and other crops, and improved farming methods. In the fifty years of Japanese rule, Taiwan became a prosperous colony in the Japanese Empire. Taipei even received electric lighting, making Taiwan only the second country in Asia to use the new technology to combat the darkness.

During World War II, Allied bombing of major ports and factories sent the economy reeling. When the Nationalists arrived in 1945, they inherited an economy largely shattered by war. To make matters worse for the island, the Nationalists shipped raw materials and industrial machinery from Taiwan to China to support the war effort against the Communists. As a result, much of Taiwan's industrial progress halted, and the Taiwanese fell back on more traditional industries, such as farming, fishing, and smaller-scale manufacturing.

Land Reform

Once Chiang Kai-shek and the Nationalist government moved to Taiwan, however, the economy began to improve slowly. The Nationalist government relied on some innovative economic thinkers and adopted some policies that quickly stimulated the local economy and led to increased prosperity. Perhaps no policy was as important in the early days as land reform. The redistribution of land

Agriculture was the most important aspect of Taiwan's economy in the 1950s. Here, a peasant plows a rice paddy with a water buffalo.

freed up capital and provided a foundation for Taiwan's "economic miracle."

In the 1950s, the early days of Nationalist rule, agriculture formed the backbone of Taiwan's economy. Rice farming, the cultivation of tea, the harvesting and processing of sugar, and the export of fruits and vegetables were mainstays of the economy. The subtropical and tropical fruit of the island became famous throughout the region. So abundant was the banana crop, for example, that Taiwan became known as the banana kingdom.

Wealth generated by agriculture, however, was unevenly distributed. A small number of large landowners controlled most of Taiwan's farms, plantations, and fruit orchards. They operated their estates on a feudal system whereby the tenants were required to hand over as much as half of their crops to the landlord. Because agriculture relies partly on the whims of nature, the harvest was uneven year to year. Years in which crops were small caused many tenant farmers to go into debt to the landlords, who could then claim a greater percentage of their crops in the future as interest on back rent. This system enriched the landlords but left many tenant farmers in a state of servitude.

To modernize the agricultural sector and encourage a diversification of the economy, the Nationalist government instituted sweeping land-reform policies in three phases. In the first phase, the government reduced the percentage of the annual yield that landholders could take as rent from their tenant farmers, allowing the farmers to accumulate their own wealth. In the second phase, the Nationalist government redistributed land that it had taken over from the Japanese colonial government. The Japanese had owned large tracts of arable land in Taiwan, and the Nationalists distributed this land in small parcels and at low prices to local farmers, who were thus given the chance to become self-supporting entrepreneurs. Finally, the government limited the size of large farms, forcing many large landholders to sell their surplus land to the government, which then redistributed the land through public auctions.

These reforms, which lasted throughout the 1950s, shattered the feudal landlord system and gave small farmers a chance to own their own farms. The policies also turned many landlords into budding capitalists. Because their landholdings were reduced, they were less tied to the land. And because the government had paid a fair price for the lands, the landlords were flush with money, which in many cases they used to modernize their farms or to invest in other enterprises.

Taiwan's land-reform policies, still studied by developing countries as a model for economic modernization, spurred the economy in new directions. Farms became more productive, but more importantly, money was invested in the creation of factories that manufactured simple products, such as plastic toys and bicycles. By the 1960s farming had fallen to just under 30 percent of the gross domestic product, and today accounts for only 2 percent of the economic output of the country.

Manufacturer for the Global Market

The growth of manufacturing caused a tremendous economic shift in Taiwan. Within two decades, the country moved from a reliance on a farming economy to one of the world's leading manufacturers. Foreign companies took advantage of the inexpensive labor and low tax rates in Taiwan to set up factories there. By the 1970s Taiwan was the second most industrialized nation in Asia after Japan. And with growth rates in the industrial sector at around 18 percent, Taiwan was hailed as one of the "tiger economies" of Asia, growing at a rate faster than most Western countries had during their periods of industrialization.

A major factor in Taiwan's industrialization was U.S. financial aid and assistance with technical training, which helped Taiwan establish an industrial infrastructure and provided people with much-needed skills to operate factories. The Taiwanese quickly mastered techniques to manufacture simple products, but they lacked the know-how to engage in heavy industry, such as the manufacture of the machinery that makes other machinery, aeronautics, petrochemicals, and projects to generate energy for the island's growing industrial sector. U.S. advisers from both the government and private sectors helped bridge this knowledge and skills gap.

At the same time, U.S. money was being funneled to the Taiwanese government, which in turn hired many of Taiwan's leading chemists, engineers, and economists to work directly for government-funded programs intended to rapidly build Taiwan's economy.

"Made in Taiwan"

During the 1960s and 1970s, when children across the Western world staged mock battles with little green army men and took their bicycles for a spin around the neighborhood, they might have noticed the small writing on the products that read "Made in Taiwan." This tag reflected an enormous shift in the Taiwanese economy, from an economy based on agriculture to one based on manufacturing.

Foreign businesses were lured to Taiwan because of the cheap labor of Taiwanese factories, the strong work ethic, and its capability for producing inexpensive products rapidly and in great quantity. Government policy encouraged growth by keeping tax rates low and offering incentives to foreign businesses to use Taiwanese manufacturers. Taiwan, in short, became a manufacturing house for the world—at least for inexpensive products.

Taiwan's manufacturers brought great wealth to the island and wages steadily climbed, as did the standard of living and education levels. By the 1980s, Taiwan was becoming an expensive place to make cheap products, but Taiwan adapted by providing a highly educated workforce to manufacture more expensive high-tech products such as microchips, fiber optics, and computer hardware. Today Taiwanese companies are designing their own products and starting to sell them under their own brand names. The tag "Made in Taiwan" is being replaced by a new label: "Made by Taiwan."

The combination of American aid and technical training and Taiwanese central government initiatives was so successful that when U.S. aid to Taiwan ended in 1964, Taiwan's economy continued to expand. The Taiwanese had a sound industrial and manufacturing base to continue on their own. By the 1980s government projects had led to the creation of petrochemical plants that proved to be enormously profitable for Taiwan and marked a step forward in its industrialization process. With government support, capital-intensive industries opened. These new industries relied on a well-educated workforce and promised greater financial rewards, but they involved a much longer period of time before the rewards were realized.

The government's role in creating the new industries was pivotal. Not only did the government support the new enterprises financially, but it also often directed research through government-run bodies that brought together scientists, academics, and entrepreneurs. The results of the government-sponsored programs were impressive. Taiwanese companies shifted from producing calculators to computers, from bicycles to computer hardware and microchips, and from textiles to fiber optics. Today Taiwan is the world's leading producer of microchips, which are used in a myriad of modern products from computers to washing machines.

Technicians work at a semiconductor facility. Taiwan is the world's leading producer of microchips.

New Political Voices

The rapid modernization of the Taiwanese economy led to a huge surge in wealth for the Taiwanese people and to dramatic social changes. The diminishing importance of farming to the economy prompted more people to move to cities in search of work. People had more money to spend and more leisure time. They began to see more movies, buy more consumer products, and read more newspapers. The government's economic programs had by and large led to prosperity, and the Taiwanese enjoyed a much better life than they had a few decades earlier.

Along with the prosperity came calls for greater political participation. At the local level, a new generation of Taiwanese politicians began to challenge the ruling Nationalist Party in local elections. And new publications appeared to voice opposition to government policies and to call for greater freedom of speech and democratization. *Formosa* magazine, for example, became a leading forum for opponents of the government. These new publications competed with Nationalist-controlled media organs, which included television, radio, newspapers, magazines, and books.

To control the new forces in Taiwan's local politics, the Nationalist Party cultivated its own opposition parties—the Young China Party and the China Democratic Socialist Party—over which it kept tight control. These parties, however, never drew wide popular support.

The rise of political opposition outside the control of the Nationalist Party, or Kuomintang (KMT) represented a far more important step in the development of Taiwan's democratization process. These new political groups gathered under the loose title of *tangwai,* a term that means "outside the party," to indicate that they offered starkly different views from the ruling KMT.

Tangwai activists staged public protests, published political journals, and drew support from long-dormant voices in cities and villages throughout Taiwan. Because it was illegal to form political parties under the martial law restrictions, the *tangwai* supported candidates standing for election as independents. By the 1980s these activists openly campaigned for candidates trying to unseat KMT incumbents.

Tangwai opposition politicians presented voters with an entirely different agenda from the KMT's. Although their members had diverse views, their defining objectives were an end to

The Kaohsiung Incident

If there is one historical incident that still simmers in Taiwan's national politics, it is the Kaohsiung Incident.

On December 10, 1979, a group of political activists gathered in the southern port city of Kaohsiung for International Human Rights Day. The rally was organized by a leading opposition journal, *Formosa,* which advocated an opening of the political system and the inclusion of more native-born Taiwanese in the national government. The activists wanted the Nationalist government to allow other political parties to form and to end the restrictions on speech and gatherings. They wanted an end to martial law and democratic reform. The protesters received permission to stage the rally from Garrison Command, the military body that enforced martial law in Taiwan. Fearing that the rally would grow too large, however, Garrison Command rescinded permission, but the protesters gathered anyway.

During the rally, some of the protesters, who some believe were police-planted provocateurs, attacked the police. In the riot that followed, scores of policemen and protesters were injured. In response to the incident, the government court-martialed and imprisoned eight people, who became known in the press as the Kaohsiung Eight. Many of the leading activists in the rally went on to form the Democratic Progressive Party (DPP), which is the ruling party of Taiwan today. A list of their names reads like a who's who of the present government and includes the vice president, Annette Lu; the president of the Control Yuan (one of the five branches of the central government); three former DPP chairmen; one DPP legislator; the Council of Labor Affairs chairwoman; and a theologian. The lawyer who represented the Kaohsiung Eight was Chen Shui-bian, the current president of the Republic of China.

Once in power, DPP members pushed for a release of classified documents relating to the incident. In March 2003 many of the declassified government documents were exhibited pub-

martial law and the establishment of a true multiparty democracy. *Tangwai* activists also called for greater emphasis on environmental reforms, greater respect for aboriginal peoples, a proclamation of independence for the island, and leadership by politicians born in Taiwan. Whereas the KMT leaders still kept one eye on the situation in China, nursing their dream of

licly in Taipei. Some opposition figures accused the DPP of releasing the documents to try to influence the presidential election, which was just a year away. Among those who would be running for office was James Soong, who had been involved in the Kaohsiung Incident, but on the side of the government. Soong at that time had been the head of the Government Information Office and was therefore responsible for publicly defending the actions of the government during the Kaohsiung Incident. Soong, now head of the People First Party, ran as an independent candidate against Chen Shui-bian in 2000 and has already announced his candidacy as a vice presidential candidate for the 2004 elections on a combined ticket with KMT running mate Lien Chan. Soong will be running against the incumbent, Chen Shui-bian.

A peaceful protest turns violent in Kaohsiung on December 10, 1979.

returning to the mainland, most of these new opposition politicians wanted nothing to do with mainland China and advocated independence for Taiwan.

Chiang Ching-kuo Ends Martial Law

The Nationalist government reacted to the growing calls for democracy and the rise of political opposition with a two-pronged approach. First, it used repression and the sweeping powers of martial law to stifle the growth of opposition. Military police and other security agencies kept files on opponents of the government and arrested many of them for sedition. Many *tangwai* politicians spent time in prison for their views, and others went abroad to carry on their work beyond the reach of the Nationalist police.

While the Nationalists clung to power through the enforcement of martial law, they also carried forward the early stages of reform that the opposition had been calling for. This liberalization of the political environment accelerated rapidly after the death of Chiang Kai-shek in 1975. In accordance with the constitution, Chiang was replaced by the vice president, Yen Chia-kan, but the real power rested in the hands of Chiang's son, Chiang Ching-kuo, who held the position of premier. In 1978 Yen stepped aside and Chiang Ching-kuo was elected president, legitimizing his already supreme position in the political hierarchy of the KMT.

Chiang Ching-kuo proved to be a much more politically open figure than his father. Although he personally controlled a vast web of secret police and other security organizations that kept a tight lid on political opposition, he accelerated the process of drawing local Taiwanese into the government to replace the many mainland politicians who were seen as having a monopoly on power. By the end of his ten years as president, Chiang Ching-kuo had raised the number of local Taiwanese in the government to reflect the number of local Taiwanese in the population of the island.

Chiang proved to be a remarkably popular president. He lacked the stiff, imperial manner of his father, favoring instead

From left to right, Chiang Kai-shek, his wife, Madame Chiang Kai-shek, and Chiang Ching-kuo, the generalissimo's son from an earlier marriage.

the smiling demeanor of a populist president. He adopted an informal style, often driving himself around Taiwan and visiting all parts of the island to hear for himself what the people thought. His policies reflected his natural inclination toward openness. He relaxed restrictions on the press and allowed for opinions critical of the government to be published.

The Long Political Journey of Chiang Ching-kuo

Chiang Ching-kuo, the eldest son of Chiang Kai-shek and president of the Republic of China from 1978 to 1988, is today credited by the majority of Taiwanese with creating Taiwan's modern economy and freeing the political system from the grip of martial law. He is also one of the most complicated figures in Taiwanese history.

After being raised in Hsikou, the family village in China's Zhejiang province, Chiang Ching-kuo, at the age of sixteen, was sent by his father for studies in the Soviet Union. It might seem odd that the right-wing generalissimo Chiang Kai-shek, who was bitterly opposed to communism and eventually fought the Chinese Communist Party in a civil war, should send his son and political heir to the word's leading Communist state. However, the Soviets had long supported the Nationalists—supplying them with weapons and advisers. According to the doctrines of Marxism and Stalinism, the Soviets believed that society must pass through a capitalist phase before achieving a Communist society based on an urban working class—the proletariat, in Communist lingo. The Soviets believed that the Nationalists could carry through this phase of development and therefore supported the Nationalists over the Chinese Communist Party, whose ideas the Soviets distrusted.

In Moscow, where Chiang Ching-kuo attended the recently established Sun Yat-sen University with other Chinese overseas students, he soaked up Communist ideology. Chiang came to believe that China's ongoing revolution must end in commu-

When, on September 28, 1986, the Democratic Progressive Party (DPP) publicly announced the formation of its party in violation of the national security laws, the reaction from the president was startling: He did nothing. The new party became the chief opposition to the KMT. A year later, Chiang Ching-kuo gave legal approval to the new party and rescinded the martial law statutes, ending the rigid political control that had been enforced since the arrival of the Nationalist troops in 1945.

nism to free the Chinese people from the tyranny of rich bankers, landlords, and capitalists of all kinds. This view was at odds with his father's dream for China. When Chiang Kai-shek attempted to destroy the Chinese Communist Party, Chiang Ching-kuo denounced him from Moscow. The story made for good copy in the newspapers, which reported the disobedience of this Chinese son.

In 1937 Chiang Ching-kuo returned to China with a Russian bride. His father dismissed his son's Communist views as the mistakes made by an impressionable youngster. He also attempted to bring Chiang Ching-kuo around to the Nationalist way of thinking and appointed him to a number of posts in the Nationalist military regime. Chiang Ching-kuo abandoned his earlier beliefs and adopted the Nationalist cause as his own, but he retained a remarkable streak of left-leaning tendencies and a passion for political reform.

As president of the Republic of China, Chiang Ching-kuo lived a simple life, shunning the imperial symbols that his father had used to rule the nation. He lived in a simple house and often drove himself around Taipei to meetings. He traveled to all parts of Taiwan, meeting local people and hiking through the countryside. Chiang Ching-kuo seemed to be a genuine man of the people, both humble and open to their concerns. He later released the government from control by the mainland Chinese who had arrived in 1945 and ended martial law. Before he died, Chiang Ching-kuo indicated that he wanted a non-mainlander to become president after his death, something for which local people had been hoping for decades. He was succeeded by Lee Teng-hui, the first president of the Republic of China to be born in Taiwan.

Lee Teng-hui

One of Chiang Ching-kuo's final acts before his death in 1988 was to indicate his preference for a tall, gregarious native-born Taiwanese named Lee Teng-hui to act as his successor for the leadership of the Nationalist Party. The act was of momentous significance. Because Lee was not a mainlander, he had no ambition to struggle for a return to China. He was educated in Japan and the United States and represented a new strain of KMT politicians who wanted to open Taiwan's political system even further and promote Taiwan on the national stage as an independent country.

Some high-ranking KMT supporters attempted to deny that Lee was Chiang Ching-kuo's choice as successor, but in a dramatic party vote Lee secured the confidence of the KMT and became the first KMT president who had been born in Taiwan. Lee, moreover, felt more comfortable speaking in his native Taiwanese dialect of Chinese than in Mandarin Chinese. He was said, in fact, to be more comfortable speaking Japanese than Mandarin as well, a fact that greatly irritated old KMT stalwarts who wanted to see Taiwan preserve the use of Mandarin as a national dialect.

If anyone doubted that Lee was going to shake up the system, they had their answer when he instituted a number of reforms to the basic structure of the ROC government on Taiwan. Lee first asked politicians who had been elected in mainland China and were still serving in Taiwan to step down. These politicians, known as the senior parliamentarians, had been separated from their constituents since 1949, when the government removed to Taiwan. Opposition politicians frequently attacked them as not representing the reality of the ROC's limited territory (Taiwan and the offshore islands). Moreover, the senior parliamentarians faced no elections; they were simply frozen in office until the Nationalist government returned to the mainland. This fact irritated many in Taiwan, who viewed it as undemocratic and outdated. In 1991 elections open to opposition candidates as well as KMT candidates were held to fill the seats in the National Assembly and legislature left by the retiring senior parliamentarians.

As president, Lee reformed other aspects of the political structure. Until Lee came into office, Taiwan had been ruled by the national government and a provincial government. The provincial government was intended to govern the island if the national government moved back to China. The two government structures overlapped in many areas of the island administration and resulted in bureaucratic waste. Lee phased out most of the powers of the provincial government and made the national government more responsive to the voters in Taiwan. Most significantly, he secured support for direct presidential elections so that voters could choose their national leader.

Lee himself ran as the incumbent in the first direct presidential election in 1996 and was returned to office with 54 percent of the vote. Observers hailed Lee as the first democratically

Lee Teng-hui (right) sits with Chen Shui-bian at a celebration in Taipei in 2002.

elected president in Chinese history. Not only had Lee won in open elections, but he had also proven that the KMT could win an election by democratic means. After nearly fifty years of ruling the island as a dictatorial power, the KMT could claim to represent the people of Taiwan as a democratically elected government in internationally monitored elections. Lee had made history for both the Republic of China and the political party that he represented.

Opposition in Power

As president, Lee played out one final act in his official political career. As the elections of 2000 approached, the KMT expected a better showing from the main opposition party, the DPP. The DPP had been slowly gaining support throughout Taiwan and had a strong support base in the south of the country. Its candidate, Chen Shui-bian, promised a responsible approach to China, helping defuse fears that a DPP election could spark war in the Taiwan Strait.

Lee supported as his successor for the KMT nomination Vice President Lien Chan, who had served loyally and worked his way up the ranks of the KMT. Lee's choice caused a rift in the party. Many KMT party members did not feel that Lien was a strong enough candidate. He lacked the popularity of the political heavyweight James Soong. On hearing of Lee's backing of Lien, Soong left the KMT and announced his bid for the presidency as an independent candidate. Soong had gained a wide base of support when he served as provincial governor of Taiwan, and he had the fiery presence of a natural populist.

Soong attacked Lien fiercely and accused the KMT of cronyism; the KMT launched reprisal attacks accusing Soong of having taken millions in party money with him when he left the KMT. The fight between Soong and Lien split KMT votes. When the final tally was taken, the DPP emerged from the three-man race as the ruling power, marking the first transfer of power to an opposition party in the history of the Republic of China.

Many KMT supporters blamed the loss on Lee Teng-hui for choosing unwisely and causing party unity to crumble. Lee eventually left the KMT and founded his own party—the Taiwan Solidarity Movement—to push for, among other things, the independence of Taiwan.

The new president, Chen Shui-bian, however, tacked in the opposite direction. Although Chen and the majority of his party were on record as supporting a declaration of independence for Taiwan, he was aware that he had not won a majority of votes in the election. Because votes were split among three candidates, Chen did not have the support of the majority of Taiwanese voters even though he had been elected president. Chen, therefore, downplayed the DPP's long struggle for a proclamation of independence.

Another reason that Chen backed away from his party's independence position was opposition to independence from the United States, Taiwan's chief military ally. A declaration of independence could trigger an invasion from mainland China, which had always threatened to use force to reunite Taiwan with the mainland if the Republic of China issued an official declaration of independence. If China attacked, the United States might well intervene on Taiwan's behalf, so the Americans were pressuring Chen not to declare independence.

The dilemma underscored the fact that Chen Shui-bian would have to shepherd the DPP into its first four-year term in the presidential office while balancing the Taipei-Washington-Beijing triangle, which could determine the ultimate fate of Taiwan as an island nation or a part of mainland China.

The election of an opposition politician to the presidency in 2000 was the result of decades of political struggle. The evolution of the political system had been fairly smooth and largely peaceful. Taiwan's political liberalization had grown out of its rapid economic growth. It seemed that on the surface all was well in the country, but the fact remained that Taiwan was still not recognized as a country by most of the world, and the population was divided over what kind of relationship Taiwan should have with China.

In Search of Normalcy 5

Perhaps there is no greater dream in Taiwan today than to enjoy the island's recent prosperity against a backdrop of longed-for political stability. Taiwan, which has made so much progress economically and politically, is still searching for a sense of normalcy. Citizens still emigrate if given a chance or send their children abroad to study and make a new life because of Taiwan's lack of long-term stability. The uncertain relationship with China lies at the heart of the problem. The situation exists in a deadlock today because public opinion is divided. Some want to proclaim independence, and some want to rejoin China. Still many others want to wait and see what happens before making a permanent arrangement.

In the meantime, the Taiwanese are searching for normalcy. They want to be citizens of a recognized country and not have to constantly explain that Taiwan is not ruled by China today, as so many people mistakenly believe. There is a great national obsession with the identity of the citizens of Taiwan, and the many questions that the Taiwanese grapple with indicate the complexity of the question of national identity even among the Taiwanese themselves. Are they Chinese people or Taiwanese people? Do they have a culture distinct from China? If not, does that mean that they are not free to break away? Can one be proud of being of Chinese heritage and still be proud of being Taiwanese?

These questions lie at the center of a great national debate in Taiwan. The Taiwanese, who have made such strong political and economic progress, are still a people trying to determine their place in the world.

The Abandonment of "One-China"
Even as the general population debates the question of Taiwan's future, Taiwanese leaders are moving forward with their poli-

cies. The administration of Chen Shui-bian, for example, has continued a policy started under former president Lee Teng-hui of promoting Taiwan as an independent power without proclaiming independence. It is a strategy fraught with danger because it tests the patience of China and the United States, which both encourage Taiwan not to move toward independence. Taiwan's relationship with China is still the paramount issue facing Taiwan, and managing the Taipei-Washington-Beijing triangle has taken up a good deal of the attentions of all the leaders of the Republic of China.

Ever since the death of Chiang Kai-shek and the democratic reforms under Chiang Ching-kuo, the long-standing Nationalist dream of retaking the mainland has been fading. Taiwan's view of its relations with mainland China first began a radical shift under the independent-minded leadership of Lee Teng-hui, who was president from 1988 to 2000. During his time as president, Lee officially renounced the patriotic obligation to retake mainland China, thereby abandoning the Republic of China's fiction of representing all of China from its temporary capital at Taipei. Continuing in this vein, Lee indicated in a number of statements that he was abandoning the "one-China" policy that allowed both Beijing and Taipei to claim to represent all of China.

The changes had tremendous implications for the international relations of the Republic of China. Lee's remarks caused alarm in both Washington and Beijing. The United States was particularly upset that Lee was abandoning the central position of U.S.-China policy without consultation. The one-China principle, no matter how much it relied on the impossible premise that two governments represented one country, created stability in the Taiwan Strait. To express its displeasure with Lee's independent action and to reassure Beijing that the United States was not involved with Lee's decision, President Bill Clinton called his counterpart in Beijing in July 1999, which helped reduce tensions in the Taiwan Strait, according to a news report in Singapore's *Straits Times:*

Three Little Links

Taiwan has had no official links with mainland China since 1949, when the Nationalist government retreated to Taiwan. On both sides of the Taiwan Strait, however, people have been clamoring for direct business, transportation, and mail routes—together known as the "three links."

A boat pulls away from the dock at Jinmen, en route to Xiamen.

Both sides agree that the three links would be good for business. Moreover, they would ease communications and travel between the two sides. Nonetheless, a myriad of problems have prevented the implementation of the three links. The obstacles include everything from security concerns—the Taiwanese feel that to open their airports to Chinese flights could aid the Chinese in an attempt to retake the island—to questions of protocol. Neither side is prepared to allow planes or ships adorned with the national flag of the other to enter its airports or harbors.

On January 1, 2001, Taiwan and China agreed to an experimental miniature of the three links. They agreed to open direct business, transportation, and postal links between Taiwan's islands of Matsu and Jinmen and China's port cities of Xiamen and Mawei. The restored contacts became known as the "three little links," and today ferries and mail boats make regular visits between the Taiwanese islands and the Chinese coast. The mini-links have legitimized the formerly illegal boat trips that used to make the short crossing and have slightly revived the economies of Taiwan's offshore islands.

In 2003 a Taipei bank representative traveled to Jinmen to investigate a surge of sales in lottery tickets on the island. He discovered that mainland residents were making the crossing to participate in the Taiwanese lottery (which offered a much higher jackpot and better odds than the lottery in China). The bank has since promised to honor winning tickets held by mainland residents, though the residents have a difficult time traveling to Taipei to collect the winnings. For that, they might have to wait for the opening of the three big links.

United States President Bill Clinton's telephone call to his Chinese counterpart Jiang Zemin—in which he reiterated Washington's commitment to the "one-China" policy—went a long way to help defuse cross-strait tension and might even make Beijing reconsider the need for a military response against Taiwan.

It showed that the US had nothing to do with Taiwan president Lee Teng-hui's redefinition of the island's status. China has been suspicious of American backing for Mr. Lee. [9]

Taiwan Rejects China's "One Country, Two Systems" Model

Lee's abandonment of the one-China policy came at a time when the Chinese government was encouraging a rise in nationalism, in part stoked by the return of two former European colonies to the government in Beijing. In 1997 Hong Kong, a remarkably prosperous island colony of Great Britain, was returned to China.

Hong Kong celebrates its return to Chinese control with a massive fireworks display.

The British had ruled the colony since the mid–nineteenth century, when they had wrested it from the Ch'ing dynasty. Beijing hoped the successful capitalist economy of Hong Kong would enrich the mainland economy, which was in the process of adopting elements of capitalism. Beijing saw it as cause for national celebration—both because China would have access to its wealth and because it helped close the historical wound of having a foreign power occupy part of its territory. The return of Hong Kong was followed in 1999 by the handover by the Portuguese of their colony of Macao, a city in Canton province that had been ruled by the Portuguese since the sixteenth century.

To avoid destroying the vibrant capitalist economies of the two former European colonies, officials in Beijing adopted a system of rule known as "one country, two systems," which would attempt to preserve the local systems while adding a layer of Chinese rule at the very top. The former colonies, in other words, would have a great deal of independence that was not allowed on the mainland.

The return of the former colonies proved to be remarkably popular in China, but for Taiwan it proved to be a dark omen because the Chinese declared that they next wanted to apply the system to Taiwan. In a speech celebrating the return of Macao to Chinese control, Chinese president Jiang Zemin declared that

> the implementation of the concept of "one country, two systems" in Hong Kong and Macau has played and will continue to play an important exemplary role for our eventual settlement of the Taiwan question. The Chinese government and people are confident and capable of an early settlement of the Taiwan question and a complete national reunification. [10]

In response, the Taiwanese soundly rejected the "one country, two systems" model for reunification with China. And to emphasize the point, Lee Teng-hui stated that Taiwan would only discuss reunification with China after China instituted democratic reforms.

The situation in the Taiwan Strait continued to be tense throughout the early days of Chen Shui-bian's election. China had always threatened to use military force to retake Taiwan if it declared independence. The election of a DPP politician to the presidency in 2000 further alarmed China. The DPP had advocated independence for Taiwan, and in 2002 Chen characterized relations between Taiwan and China as relations between "countries" on the two sides of the Taiwan Strait. In essence, Chen was repeating Lee's description of Taiwan as an independent political entity, though he denied that it amounted to a statement of independence for Taiwan. But the Chinese reaction to Chen's statement indicated that the Chinese had adopted a new strategy to bring Taiwan back under Chinese control: They would be patient. Threats of war had not succeeded in intimidating Taiwanese voters, and China chose to emphasize peaceful reunification to warm the Taiwanese to the possibility of eventually returning to China.

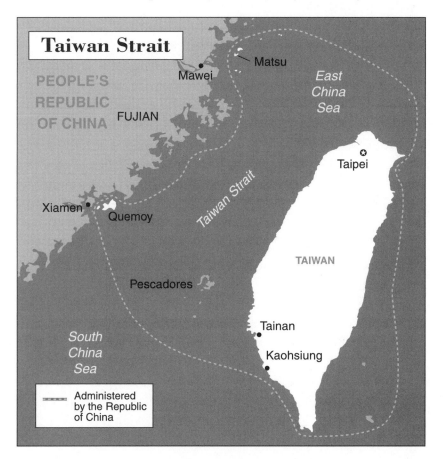

On the verge of retirement, Chinese premier Zhu Rongji, in his final report to the National People's Congress in March 2003, adopted the new, softer tone when mentioning Taiwan: "We must implement the basic principles of peaceful reunification," he said, "and strive for an early resumption of dialogue and negotiation between the two sides."[11] The Chinese premier also referred to Taiwan and China as "two countries" but corrected his phrasing shortly after by calling them the "two sides."

The change in tone from Beijing's leaders, however, does not indicate that they have abandoned their long-stated desire of returning Taiwan to rule by the mainland. And to keep pressure on the Taiwanese, the People's Liberation Army has stationed batteries of missiles across the Taiwan Strait in the province of Fujian aimed at targets in Taiwan.

The Middle Way

Unrecognized by most of the world as a sovereign state and claimed by the People's Republic of China as a province of its own, Taiwan remains in a dangerous situation that places great restrictions on Taiwan's leaders in guiding their international policy. Chen Shui-bian has adopted the "middle way" in relations with China, neither declaring independence for Taiwan nor moving toward reunification. But Chen's policy has alienated some of the core supporters of the DPP and underscores the fact that Taiwan's democracy is still in its early phases. Sheng Lijun, a scholar writing about Taiwan, describes the competing demands placed on Chen as the national leader of Taiwan and the head of a political party that has espoused independence:

Taiwan's independence and democracy were core and life-long pursuits for only some DPP leaders. To the rest, they were only political convenience to obtain state power. In other words, while they were the ends for some leaders, they were the means for the other. Grasping state power was the only aim all the factions shared, which accounted heavily for their unity. Once in power, however, factional differences and tension have developed rapidly. The appeal of democracy, though effective in the past, cannot be used now as the KMT is no longer the ruling party. And the Chen Shui-bian government cannot openly appeal for Taiwan independence due to Chinese and international pressures, and has to claim to move from the "left" to the "middle of the road." The result is confusion among those Taiwan independence advocators and loss of their support. [12]

To counter criticisms that Chen has abandoned the independence plank in the DPP's platform, Chen has resorted to more subtle methods to ensure the independence of Taiwan from mainland rule. These efforts fall generally into two categories: a cultural and educational shift toward a Taiwan-centered identity and economic policies that encourage a reduced dependence on China.

Education

When the Nationalist government arrived in Taiwan, it implemented a school system that focused on China in key subjects, such as history, geography, and literature. The 85 percent of the population of Taiwan that had been living in Taiwan for centuries found itself switching from the Japanese educational system to the Nationalist Chinese system. In geography classes, for instance, Taiwanese students had to identify the provinces and provincial capitals of the Chinese mainland and describe the topography of different regions that were far from their homes in Taiwan. And in history and literature courses, Taiwan was usually mentioned only briefly and sometimes not at all.

Government examinations, administered by the Examination Yuan for entry to civil service jobs, required a detailed knowledge of Chinese geography, history, and civilization. In the early decades of the Nationalist government's rule, this system ensured that government officials would have suitable background knowledge to carry on their duties if the government returned to the mainland.

Taiwan's Political Parties

Since the end of martial law in Taiwan in 1987, a number of political parties have arisen, giving Taiwanese voters a greater selection of candidates and political platforms from which to choose. The following are the five largest political parties in Taiwan today.

Democratic Progressive Party (DPP). Founded a year before the end of martial law, the DPP arose in opposition to the then-ruling Kuomintang (KMT). The DPP drew supporters from among the ranks of the *tangwai,* or opposition activists.

The DPP platform traditionally included an independence plank, but since DPP politician Chen Shui-bian was elected to the presidency in 2000, he has moved away from declaring independence to preserve stability in the Taiwan Strait. The DPP still struggles for political reform of the government and promotes the Republic of China as "Taiwan" so that it is not mistaken abroad for the People's Republic of China. The DPP is also considered the "greenest" party because of its advocacy of environmental legislation and its opposition to the expansion of Taiwan's nuclear facilities.

Kuomintang (KMT). Also known as the Nationalist Party, the KMT was once synonymous with the government of the Republic of China. It first set up a republican government in Nanjing in 1911 and ruled Taiwan for fifty years, mostly under martial law, before losing the presidency in 2000 in a multiparty election.

The KMT has traditionally drawn support from the Chinese immigrants who arrived in Taiwan after 1945. It is estimated to be the world's richest political party and has always had among its ranks some of the richest citizens of Taiwan. The KMT is in the process of trying to divest itself of its many financial enterprises and rebuild itself as a modern political party to win back the presidency in the 2004 presidential election. It is today the chief opposition party in Taiwan, and the KMT chairman, Lien

The Nationalist government also promoted Taiwan as the protector of Chinese civilization while the Communists on the mainland sought to destroy many historical legacies of the Chinese. During the Cultural Revolution of the late 1960s and early 1970s, the Red Guards, the vanguard of the movement, smashed Bud-

Chan, has already received his party's support as the presidential candidate.

People First Party (PFP). The PFP is the creation of James Soong, former provincial governor of Taiwan and longtime KMT member. During the run-up to the 2000 presidential elections, Soong left the KMT after the party chose Lien Chan as its presidential nominee. Soong ran as an independent and outpolled the KMT's candidate but lost by less than 3 percentage points to DPP candidate Chen Shui-bian.

After the elections, Soong formed the PFP. In March 2003, however, Soong forged an alliance with the KMT and announced a joint PFP-KMT ticket for the 2004 elections, with Soong as the vice presidential candidate and KMT chairman Lien Chan as the presidential candidate.

New Party (NP). The NP broke away from the KMT in 1993 to rally support for an anticorruption and socially progressive platform. The NP favors the immediate opening of direct air and shipping links with China and eventual political reunification. It draws much of its support from the offshore islands of Quemoy, Matsu, and the Pescadores, which all stand a good chance of benefiting economically from a reopening of trade across the Taiwan Strait. The New Party is the smallest member of a legislative voting bloc known as the "pan-blue alliance," which also includes the KMT and the PFP.

Taiwan Solidarity Union (TSU). Taiwan's newest political force, the TSU, formed in 2001. Its founder and leading advocate is former Republic of China president Lee Teng-hui. Lee left the KMT to form the TSU to promote a strong local identity for the Taiwanese (partly by advocating the use of the local dialects of Chinese, as opposed to Mandarin, the dialect predominantly spoken in China) and to work toward independence for the island. The TSU has drawn supporters from the ranks of the KMT and the DPP who favor Taiwan's independence. The TSU is generally closer to the DPP in the legislature, and the two parties often work together in what is known as the "pan-green alliance."

dhist and Confucian temples and even desecrated the grave of Confucius.

Many Taiwanese watched in horror as the legacies of their civilization were destroyed in an ideological frenzy. And while the Communists condemned their historical cultural heritage, Taiwan became the refuge of the old ways. The Taiwanese, for example, still use the traditional Chinese writing system, whereas the Communists had simplified it to improve literacy. They have also preserved the complicated grammatical usages and aphorisms employed in formal essay writing, and today Taiwanese newspaper editorials are considered among the most difficult to read in the Chinese-speaking world.

By the 1990s, when Lee Teng-hui had renounced ambitions to retake China, a lively debate arose about the usefulness of an educational system that focused primarily on China. Lee himself advocated a more local focus. "It is absurd that our curriculum in history and geography is full of stuff about China," he said. "I shall ask our schools to replace them with those of Taiwan." [13]

The debate over education proved to be emotional and revealed a rift in Taiwanese society. Some Taiwanese believed that Taiwan's greatness rested partly in the historical greatness of Chinese civilization. Members of this group wanted to continue teaching their children about their Chinese heritage. Another group wanted the curriculum to focus on Taiwan, which it felt had been overlooked for too long, but also to include a more global perspective. Many others fall somewhere between these two positions.

In 2002 the Ministry of Education announced new guidelines for public schools in Taiwan that called for a greater emphasis on Taiwan-centered education. The new guidelines encouraged the teaching of dialects of Chinese other than Mandarin for the first time in the history of the Republic of China on Taiwan. The guidelines also specified that Taiwanese literature and Taiwanese history courses should be taught. The guidelines were a clear indication that the Chen administration was pushing for a cultural perspective independent of China. It also indicated the close relationship of politics and education in Taiwan, a land that is still in the process of defining its national and cultural identity.

Economic Policy

A second focus of Chen's attempts to secure an identity separate of China can be found in his administration's economic policy.

As Taiwan prospered and local wages rose during the 1970s and 1980s, employing workers in Taiwan became more expensive. As a result, Taiwanese and foreign companies began to move their factories to Southeast Asia and China. It was in many ways a natural economic progression, and Taiwanese capitalists began to take advantage of inexpensive labor elsewhere just as foreign companies had once been drawn to Taiwan for the same reason.

By the late 1990s Taiwanese business investments began to flow rapidly into China, which had low labor costs and a government that offered a range of incentives, such as low or no taxation. The Chinese government was so eager for foreign investment that it would even upgrade infrastructure for companies setting up shop in China. If a foreign company, for example, built a factory in an undeveloped area of China, the government might sell the company the land cheaply and build a road to it at no extra cost. These policies drew a number of Taiwanese businesses to China, but even today there are no direct flights from Taiwan to China, nor are their direct shipping links. Mail between the two sides of the Taiwan Strait, for example, is diverted first to another destination, usually Hong Kong, before being delivered to its final destination. Businesspeople must also travel by the same circuitous route, and so does the great amount of investment capital passing between the two sides.

Despite having to stop at a third point on their way to China because of the ban on cross-strait transportation, Taiwanese investors found China's market too tempting to resist. But the rapid development of economic links between Taiwan and China put the Taiwanese government in a quandary. If Taiwanese businesses were so dependent on the mainland for their livelihood, would it make the Chinese goal of bringing Taiwan back under mainland rule easier? The Taiwanese government has struggled with the question ever since. On the one hand, it does not want to encourage reliance on a China that is hostile to its independence, and on the other, it does not want to dampen economic growth because of politics.

When the issue first cropped up in the 1990s, Lee Teng-hui adopted a policy of encouraging Taiwanese businesses to invest in the countries of Southeast Asia, which offered cheap labor and other benefits. Chen Shui-bian has also promoted the policy, known as the Go-South Policy, as a means of steering clear of China without hurting Taiwanese business. The Go-South Policy, however, has not deterred Taiwanese businesses from investing in China. One reason is the close cultural connections of the two sides of the Taiwan Strait. Taiwanese businessmen can speak to their counterparts in China in Chinese, and they generally feel at home in a Chinese environment that is less foreign than the environments of other countries.

The competing political and economic pressures are highlighted by Chen's statements to different constituents. When he

Chinese employees work in a Taiwanese-owned company located near Shanghai, China.

speaks to advocates of independence, he often points out that the Go-South Policy is preserving Taiwan's autonomy. But Chen has also made remarks to groups of DPP businessmen promising to ease restrictions on Taiwanese businesses moving to China and even to open direct business, mail, and transportation routes across the Taiwan Strait.

Meanwhile, to attract foreign companies to return to Taiwan, the Taiwanese government has offered a series of government incentives similar to China's. Taiwan, however, is looking for more choosey investors, such as high-tech and biotechnology firms. The theory is that because Taiwan offers a highly skilled workforce and is more politically stable than China, Taiwan can become a regional center for research and development in rapidly changing high-tech fields. Whatever the effects of Taiwan's government policies, China, as the fastest-growing economy in Asia, will most likely figure largely in Taiwan's economic life.

As Taiwan grapples with the question of its relationship with China and struggles for international recognition, Taiwanese society continues to evolve. Despite their pride in the country's political and economic advances, the Taiwanese face an uncertain future. It is not uncommon to hear people in Taiwan talking about what will happen to Taiwan, as if it might one day disappear as a recognizable place. It is hard to imagine the nationals of other countries having similar debates. There will most likely always be a Japan, a France, and an India. But will Taiwan be a nation in the future, or will it disappear into a wave of Chinese expansion?

Few nations have changed as quickly as Taiwan. Indeed, few nations have been so praised for their achievements in politics and economics. And yet even Taiwan's democratic allies refuse to support independence for the country, at least until the Taiwanese decide for themselves what kind of future they want. Despite pressure from mainland China and the United States, only the Taiwanese can decide their island's future. Until that time, Taiwan will continue to exist internationally in an odd state of official invisibility, and at home the Taiwanese will continue to debate just what it means to be Taiwanese.

Notes

Introduction: A New Democracy

1. Quoted in William Ide and Lin Chieh-yu, "New Era Begins," *Taipei Times,* May 21, 2000, p. 17.

Chapter One: On the Edge of the Middle Kingdom

2. Quoted in Jose Eugenio Borao Mateo, ed., *Spaniards in Taiwan (Documents),* vol. 1, *1582–1641.* Taipei, Taiwan: SMC, 2001, pp. 10–11.

3. George Leslie MacKay, *From Far Formosa: The Island, Its People, and Missions.* New York: Fleming H. Revell, 1895, p. 105.

Chapter Two: A Republic in Exile

4. Joseph J. Nerbonne, *A Foreign Correspondent Looks at Taiwan.* Taipei, Taiwan: Published privately, 1973, p. 86.

Chapter Three: The Other China

5. Jay Taylor, *The Generalissimo's Son: Chiang Ching-kuo and the Revolutions in China and Taiwan.* Cambridge, MA: Harvard University Press, 2000, p. 206.

6. Shelley Rigger, *Politics in Taiwan: Voting for Democracy.* New York: Routledge, 1999, pp. 106–107.

7. Quoted in *Implementation of Taiwan Relations Act: An Examination After Twenty Years.* Baltimore: University of Maryland School of Law, 2001, p. 251.

8. Charles T. Cross, *Born a Foreigner: A Memoir of the American Presence in Asia.* New York: Rowman & Littlefield, 1999, p. 257.

Chapter Five: In Search of Normalcy

9. Ching Cheong, *Will Taiwan Break Away? The Rise of Taiwanese Nationalism.* Singapore: World Scientific, 2001, p. 154.

10. Quoted in Cheong, *Will Taiwan Break Away?* p. 116.

11. Quoted in *Taipei Times,* "China and Taiwan 'Two Countries': Zhu," March 6, 2003, p. 3.

12. Quoted in John F. Copper, ed., *Taiwan in Troubled Times: Essays on the Chen Shui-bian Presidency.* Singapore: World Scientific, 2002, p. 80.

13. Quoted in Cheong, *Will Taiwan Break Away?* p. 119.

Chronology

Pre-1400s
Taiwan is inhabited by tribes of Malayo-Polynesian aborigines.

ca. 1400
Emigrants from China's Fujian province begin to settle in Taiwan.

1544
Portuguese land in Taiwan and dub it Ilha Formosa, the "Beautiful Island."

1624
The Dutch erect Fort Zeelandia on an islet, named Taiwan, close to today's Tainan City, and begin to colonize the southwestern part of the island.

1626
The Spanish settle in northern Taiwan and build Fort Santo Domingo.

1642
The Dutch expel the Spanish from northern Taiwan.

1653
The Dutch build Fort Provintia in today's Tainan City after Chinese immigrants' unsuccessful rebellion.

1661
After being defeated by Manchus in China, Koxinga, the last general of the Ming dynasty, leads twenty-five thousand nobles, soldiers, and pirates to invade Taiwan.

1662
After a siege of nine months and the loss of sixteen hundred Dutch lives, Governor Coyett surrenders Taiwan to Koxinga. Koxinga dies four months later, and his son succeeds as king of Taiwan.

1683
Manchus led by Shilang, Koxinga's former officer, annihilate the kingdom of Taiwan and annex western Taiwan to the Chinese Empire.

1867
John Dodd, a pioneer of Taiwan's tea industry, rents two clippers and begins exporting Formosa oolong to New York.

1884
French forces led by Admiral Coubert invade northern Taiwan and occupy Chi-lung.

1885
Coubert occupies the Pescadores with a vision to transform them into France's Hong Kong. In June he dies of a tropical disease. French forces withdraw from the Chi-lung area and the Pescadores.

1887
The Chinese annex Taiwan, giving it provincial status.

1895
China cedes Taiwan to Japan in the Treaty of Shimonoseki, which ends the Sino-Japanese War; the Taiwanese establish the first republic in Asia to resist impending Japanese rule.

1898
Kodama Gentaro becomes the fourth governor-general. He appoints Goto Shimpei as chief administrator. Taiwan begins its painful modernization.

1902
The legendary anti-Japanese leader Lim Siau-Niau and his followers are killed while defending their stronghold, Au Pia Na, near Kaohsiung. This marks the end of open military resistance of the Taiwanese people against Japanese rule.

1911
The Ch'ing dynasty is overthrown; the Republic of China (ROC) is established.

1927–1949
The Chinese Civil War between Chinese Nationalists and Communists occurs.

1937
Japan invades China, and World War II begins in Asia. Taiwan is an important staging area for Japanese troops.

1943
The Cairo Declaration is issued by the United States and the United Kingdom promising to "restore" Taiwan to China.

1945
World War II ends; Taiwan returns to Nationalist rule; the ROC signs the United Nations Charter and becomes a founding member of the UN.

1947
Chinese rule brings widespread corruption to the government, chaos to society, and runaway inflation to the economy. On February 28 a general uprising breaks out. Chiang Kai-shek sends in troops from China and conducts ruthless suppression. Twenty thousand Taiwanese are massacred by Nationalist troops.

1949
China's civil war ends. Nationalists flee to Taiwan; the People's Republic of China (PRC) is established; the PRC lays claim to Taiwan.

1949–1987
Chiang Kai-shek establishes martial law in Taiwan.

1950
The Korean War; the United States sends the Seventh Fleet to the Taiwan Strait.

1951
The San Francisco Peace Treaty establishes a legal basis for Taiwanese self-determination.

1971
Taiwan's seat in the UN is given to the People's Republic of China.

1972
The Shanghai Communiqué establishes normal relations between the United States and China.

1975
Chiang Kai-shek dies.

1978
Chiang Ching-kuo, Chiang Kai-shek's son, becomes president of the Republic of China.

1979
The United States recognizes the PRC and de-recognizes the ROC; the United States signs the Taiwan Relations Act to protect the welfare of Taiwan; the Kaohsiung Incident occurs; An opposition rally is violently suppressed by the Nationalists.

1980s
Chiang Ching-kuo's government focuses on development, fostering Taiwan's economic boom.

1986
The Democratic Progressive Party (DPP) is formed—Taiwan's first opposition party.

1987
Martial law is lifted.

1988
Chiang Ching-kuo dies; the KMT appoints Lee Teng-hui president of Taiwan, making him the first Taiwan-born leader of the island under the Nationalists; Taiwanese are allowed to visit mainland China for the first time in forty years.

1991
The independence platform is adopted by the DPP; the Nationalist Party abandons its claim to be the only legitimate government of China, saying instead that it leads one of two equal governments. Beijing denounces this as separatism.

1992
The DPP gains one-third of the seats in parliamentary elections.

1993
The UN rejects Taiwan's membership application.

1995
Taiwan's President Lee Teng-hui makes a private visit to Cornell University. Beijing is alarmed that a Taiwanese leader has been given a U.S. visa, and it holds missile exercises in the Taiwan Strait.

1996

Lee Teng-hui is reelected president by popular vote; China deploys one hundred and fifty thousand troops on the mainland near Taiwan and begins missile tests aimed at influencing the Taiwanese elections. The United States sends two carrier groups to the region to prevent escalation.

1998

U.S. president Bill Clinton visits China and says that the United States does not support Taiwan's independence. Some Taiwanese see Clinton's statement as damaging their right to self-determination; the Clinton administration claims there has been no change in U.S. policy toward Taiwan.

2000

Chen Shui-bian is elected president, becoming the first Taiwanese leader elected from an opposition party, thereby ending fifty years of rule by the Nationalist Party. In his first speech he abandons his party's pro-independence platform in an attempt to ease tensions with the Communist mainland.

For Further Reading

Books

Robert Green, *Modern Nations of the World: Taiwan.* San Diego: Lucent Books, 2001. A general introduction to Taiwan's geography, history, and people.

Insight Guides: Taiwan. Singapore: APA, 1998. A self-described "visual travel book," this *Insight Guide* provides essays on Taiwanese history and culture with descriptions of some central tourist sights on the island and many attractive photographs.

Eduardo del Rio (Rius), *Mao for Beginners.* New York: Pantheon Books, 1980. An entertaining and informative summary of Mao's life and his beliefs by the left-leaning Mexican journalist Rius. A simple introduction to the man who was the military and ideological rival of Chiang Kai-shek.

Sterling Seagrave, *The Soong Dynasty.* New York: Harper & Row, 1986. A revealing portrait of one of China's most influential families, with much biographical information on the rise of the Nationalist Party and Chiang Kai-shek, the founder of Taiwan.

Douglas C. Smith, *The Yami of Lan-Yu Island: Portrait of a Culture in Transition.* Bloomington, IN: Phi Delta Kappa Educational Foundation, 1998. A study of the ancient inhabitants of Lan-yu Island, off the east coast of Taiwan.

Jonathan D. Spence and Annping Chin, *The Chinese Century: A Photographic History of the Last Hundred Years.* New York: Random House, 1996. An oversize volume of photographs and essays from about 1900 to the Tiananmen Square incident, including an interesting section on the Nationalist government, which moved to Taiwan in 1949.

Robert Storey, *Taiwan*. Hawthorn, Australia: Lonely Planet, 1998. A comprehensive guidebook to Taiwan, including information on language, culture, history, and information on the surrounding islands.

Websites

Democratic Progressive Party (www.dpp.org.tw). The official website of the ruling political party in Taiwan.

Kuomintang (www.kmt.org.tw). The official website of the Nationalist Party, the chief opposition party in Taiwan.

New Party (www.np.org.tw). The website of the New Party.

People First Party (www.pfp.org.tw). The website of the People First Party.

Republic of China Government Information Office (www.gio.gov.tw). The site features general information on Taiwan, up-to-date press releases, and links to government publications.

Taiwan's 400 Years of History (www.taiwandc.org/history.htm). This website offers brief essays on different aspects of Taiwan's history and has some good links to other sites.

Taiwan Solidarity Union (www.tsu.org.tw). The website of Taiwan's newest political party.

Works Consulted

Books

Chen Shui-bian, *Facing Challenges and Forging Ahead: President Chen Shui-bian's Selected Addresses and Messages (II)*. Taipei, Taiwan: Office of the President, 2002. A collection of speeches from 2001 delivered by the president of the Republic of China and chairman of the Democratic Progressive Party.

Ching Cheong, *Will Taiwan Break Away? The Rise of Taiwanese Nationalism*. Singapore: World Scientific, 2001. A collection of newspaper articles about Taiwan by a correspondent of the *Straits Times*.

John F. Copper, *Historical Dictionary of Taiwan*. Metuchen, NJ: Scarecrow, 1993. A dictionary of modern Taiwanese figures and events, with a historical introduction and time line.

———, *Taiwan: Nation-State or Province?* Boulder, CO: Westview, 1999. A good overview of the historical, economic, and social factors that have shaped modern Taiwan and its complicated relationship with China.

John F. Copper, ed., *Taiwan in Troubled Times: Essays on the Chen Shui-bian Presidency*. Singapore: World Scientific, 2002. A collection of essays on the first year of presidential rule by the Democratic Progressive Party.

Charles T. Cross, *Born a Foreigner: A Memoir of the American Presence in Asia*. New York: Rowman & Littlefield, 1999. A memoir by a longtime American diplomat and the first director of the American Institute in Taiwan.

John King Fairbank, *The United States and China.* Cambridge, MA: Harvard University Press, 1979. A scholarly introduction to modern China and Chinese American relations.

Sven Hedin, *Chiang Kai-shek: Marshal of China.* Trans. Bernard Norbelie. New York: Da Capo, 1975. An unabashedly adulatory biography of Chiang Kai-shek.

Implementation of Taiwan Relations Act: An Examination After Twenty Years. Baltimore: University of Maryland School of Law, 2001. A collection of essays by U.S. diplomats and scholars that examines the effects of the landmark legislation that has kept the United States a close ally of Taiwan even after the severing of official relations.

George H. Kerr, *Formosa: Licensed Revolution and the Home Rule Movement, 1895–1945.* Honolulu: University of Hawaii Press, 1974. A study of the effects of Japanese occupation on Taiwan's industry and society.

The Legacy of the Taiwan Relations Act: A Compendium of Authoritative Twentieth Anniversary Assessments. Taipei, Taiwan: Government Information Office of the Republic of China, 1999. A collection of talks and essays written on the occasion of the twentieth anniversary of the signing of the act of Congress that forms a key bridge between the United States and Taiwan.

George Leslie MacKay, *From Far Formosa: The Island, Its People, and Missions.* New York: Fleming H. Revell, 1895. An account of Taiwan in the late nineteenth century by a Canadian missionary who established a Presbyterian church in the northern port city of Tansui.

Jose Eugenio Borao Mateo, ed., *Spaniards in Taiwan (Documents).* Vol. 1. *1582–1641.* Taipei, Taiwan: SMC, 2001. A collection of primary sources about the history of the Spanish interest in and presence on Taiwan.

Douglas Mendel, *The Politics of Formosan Nationalism.* Berkeley and Los Angeles: University of California Press, 1970. An examination of the rise of pro-independence nationalism in Taiwan and antimainland sentiment directed at both the Communists and the Nationalists.

Raymon H. Myers, ed., *Two Societies in Opposition: The Republic of China and the People's Republic of China After Forty Years.* Stanford, CA: Hoover Institution, 1991. A collection of essays looking at the changes in Taiwan-China relations and how the two societies have changed during their fifty years of separation.

Joseph J. Nerbonne, *A Foreign Correspondent Looks at Taiwan.* Taipei, Taiwan: Published privately, 1973. A collection of newspaper and magazine reportage by an American correspondent stationed in Taiwan.

Shelley Rigger, *Politics in Taiwan: Voting for Democracy.* New York: Routledge, 1999. An overview of the growth of the Republic of China (Taiwan) from an authoritarian state to a multiparty democracy.

Fred W. Riggs, *Formosa Under Chinese Nationalist Rule.* New York: Macmillan, 1952. A detailed study of the first decade of Nationalist rule in China.

Murray A. Rubinstein, ed., *The Other Taiwan, 1945 to the Present.* New York: M.E. Sharpe, 1994. A collection of scholarly essays on various aspects of Taiwanese society.

James E. Sheridan, *China in Disintegration: The Republican Era in Chinese History, 1912–1949.* New York: Free Press, 1975. A history of the 1911 revolution and the Chinese Civil War between the Nationalists and the Communists.

Jonathan D. Spence, *The Search for Modern China.* New York: W.W. Norton, 1990. An in-depth study of the forces that shaped modern China, from the Ming dynasty to the protests at Tiananmen Square. Its author is the most famous living China scholar writing in English.

Jay Taylor, *The Generalissimo's Son: Chiang Ching-kuo and the Revolutions in China and Taiwan.* Cambridge, MA: Harvard University Press, 2000. A biography of the son of Chiang Kai-shek, who ruled Taiwan from 1978 to 1988 and who helped democratize Taiwan's political system.

Barbara W. Tuchman, *Stilwell and the American Experience in China, 1911–45.* New York: Bantam Books, 1972. A portrait of Joe "Vinegar" Stilwell, the highest-ranking U.S. general in China during World War II and a history of American relations with the Nationalist Chinese government.

Willem Van Kemenade, *China, Hong Kong, Taiwan, Inc.* New York: Knopf, 1997. A study of the interplay between these distinct Chinese economies.

Periodicals

William Ide and Lin Chieh-yu, "New Era Begins," *Taipei Times,* May 21, 2000.

Taipei Times, "China and Taiwan 'Two Countries': Zhu," March 6, 2003.

Index

Picture Credits

Cover photo: Simon Kwong/Reuters/Landov
© AFP/CORBIS, 19
AP/Wide World Photos, 43, 67, 78
© Bettmann/CORBIS, 35
Bloomberg News/Landov, 64
Claro Cortes/Reuters/Landov, 88
Dirck Halstead/Liaison/Getty Images, 55
Hulton/Archive by Getty Images, 29, 31, 40, 52, 60, 69
Chris Jouan, 20, 81
© Catherine Karnow/CORBIS, 79
Simon Kwong/Reuters/Landov, 8, 73
Landov, 47
© Victoria & Albert Museum, London/Art Resource, NY, 23

About the Author

Robert Green is the senior editor of the *Taiwan Review*, a monthly publication of the Government Information Office of the Republic of China. He holds a master's degree in journalism from New York University and a bachelor's degree in English literature from Boston University. He first traveled to Taiwan on a Blakemore Foundation Language Grant. Among his twenty-five books are four others published by Lucent Books: *China*, *Taiwan*, and *Cambodia*, all in the Modern Nations of the World series, and *Dictators*.